KU-262-590

"The greatest thing by far is to be a master of metaphor." Aristotle

RotoVision

A RotoVision Book

Published and distributed by RotoVision SA
Route Suisse 9
CH-1295 Mies
Switzerland

RotoVision SA
Sales and Editorial Office
Sheridan House, 114 Western Road
Hove BN3 1DD, UK

Tel: +44 (0)1273 72 72 68
Fax: +44 (0)1273 72 72 69
www.rotovision.com

To my wife Dagmar in supreme
gratitude for her support,
professional advice, and long-
suffering patience; and to my
son Nicolas for his gentle
understanding while Dad
went bananas with his book.

LEARNING
RESOURCES
CENTRE

Copyright © RotoVision SA 2010
First published in hardback 2008

All rights reserved. No part of this publication may be
reproduced, stored in a retrieval system, or transmitted
in any form or by any means, electronic, mechanical,
photocopying, recording or otherwise, without
permission of the copyright holder.

While every effort has been made to contact owners
of copyright material produced in this book, we have not
always been successful. In the event of a copyright query,
please contact the Publisher.

In addition to all the individual contributors, RotoVision would like
to thank the Nike, Nokia, and Bang & Olufsen media centers for
the use of their images in this book.

10 9 8 7 6 5 4 3 2 1

ISBN: 978-2-88893-135-5

Art Director: Jane Waterhouse
Design: JCLanaway

Reprographics in Singapore by ProVision Pte. Ltd.
Tel: +65 6334 7720
Fax: +65 6334 7721

Printing and binding in Singapore by
Star Standard Industries (Pte) Ltd.

658.827

A9

302465

Issues

Anatomy

Portfolios and case studies

Etcetera

What is branding?

> "Human civilization is dependent upon signs and systems of signs, and the human mind is inseparable from the functioning of signs—if indeed mentality is not to be identified with such functioning."
>
> Charles Morris, *Foundations of the Theory of Signs*

The word "brand" comes from the Old Norse or Germanic root meaning "burn." We use this meaning literally when we talk about branding an animal, or an amphora of wine, to indicate its owner; we mean it figuratively when we talk about all the attributes of a product that make a lasting impression in a customer's mind.

Patrick Barwise, in his introduction to *The Economist*'s 2004 collection of essays *Brands and Branding*, defines three distinct things that a brand can be. The nuances of his definitions, outlined below, are important. A brand can be:

- a named product or service, such as Ivory Soap or BBC News (this refers to the branded thing itself);
- a trademark such as Panasonic or Bass (this refers to the name or symbol in the abstract sense); or
- a customer's beliefs about a product or service, epitomized by such famous phrases as "Nobody ever got fired for buying IBM." (The economic value that accrues from such implicit trust in the brand is often called brand equity.)

What can have a brand? In short, anything: products, services, organizations, places, and people. Even you.

A brand is a promise of satisfaction. It is a sign, a metaphor operating as an unwritten contract between a manufacturer and a consumer, a seller and a buyer, a performer and an audience, an environment and those who inhabit it, an event and those who experience it.

The consumer, buyer, audience, inhabitant, and "experiencer" (all customers) form their own feelings about what a brand means; but they can be influenced—more than most realize—by the advertising and publicity of the manufacturer, seller, performer, environment, or event (all producers).

Branding is the process of continuous struggle between producers and customers to define that promise and meaning. To paraphrase Karl Marx, people make their own decisions about who to be, how to live, and what to buy, but under circumstances shaped by brands' advertising, marketing, and publicity.

Most buying behavior is driven by storytelling and emotions, which are exploited by brands. How brands are created—and the process by which things are branded—is the subject of this book.

Symbol vs. brand
Visual context, story, and
emotional connections are
what distinguish a symbol
from a brand.

The components of branding

Brands arise in times of economic plenty. When there is scarcity, brands starve. The modern practice of branding got going in earnest with the Industrial Revolution (late eighteenth and early nineteenth centuries), which gave rise to surplus production and the ability to distribute goods far and wide. Corporations created brands as a way of increasing sales outside their immediate place of production. Some of the earliest goods to be branded and exported were alcoholic drinks. Some of France's greatest wineries were brand names even before the revolution. Breweries such as Guinness and Bass also trace the origins of their brands to the eighteenth century.

William Procter, a candlemaker, and James Gamble, a soapmaker, were early pioneers of branding. They went into business together in 1837, and during the American Civil War supplied the Northern armies with essentials like soap. Veterans carried awareness of Procter and Gamble's products back home. Ivory soap launched its first national advertising campaign in 1882.

Branding, as it is generally practiced today, involves five components:

- positioning;
- storytelling;
- design;
- price; and
- customer relationship.

Positioning, a concept first laid out by Al Ries and Jack Trout in their 1980 book of that name, means defining in the mind of a customer what a brand stands for and how it compares with competing brands. It is important for producers to focus on what the customer thinks, and respond to that. This is what makes branding a two-way process.

Storytelling is what humans have done for millennia. Everyone is drawn to a good, emotional story and wants to hear the best ones over and over again. When we buy brands, we take part in their story: great brands reassure us as to what an important role we play in their great story.

Design refers to all aspects of how a thing is crafted, not just the visual aspect. The design is the liquid as well as the label, the nuts and bolts as well as the name, the self as well as the surface. Often, when a company talks of rebranding, they really just mean a redesign. A true rebranding cuts to the core concept.

Price is a vital, though less obvious aspect of a brand. If two cheeses in the supermarket look and smell the same, most customers will take the more expensive one. This has been proven. Price jockeying is crucial in brand competition, and many companies have learned, to their cost, that short-term price-cutting tactics can have devastating long-term consequences for brand image.

Customer relationship management represents the sometimes quixotic efforts of corporations to make each of us feel special. This is vital. Your phone company has millions of customers, but has to make you and every other one feel like the most important. A difficult trick, but try they must.

At the heart of every branding effort there has to be a kernel of truth. The beauty of great branding lies in its ability to identify that truth, tell its story, make it look good, and build it into a valuable, emotional bond between producer and customer.

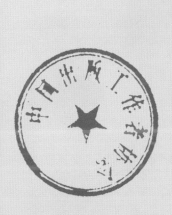

Context and meaning
What does a red star signify? That depends on what you associate it with. To some, it is a Communist symbol. To others, it is the logo of the USA's largest department store, Macy's. Yet others think of Stella Artois beer, or Eastern European football. One symbol, many brands.

What branding does

"Nothing will put a bad product out of business faster than a good advertising campaign."

Morris Hite

Branding can do several useful things, all of which help to ensure the success of the product or service. It can:

• reinforce a good reputation;
• encourage loyalty;
• assure quality;
• convey a perception of greater worth, allowing a product to be priced higher (or a product of equal price to sell more); and
• grant the buyer a sense of affirmation and entry into an imaginary community of shared values.

A brand resides primarily in the minds of customers, and is often synonymous with reputation. In other words, your brand is what your customers think it is. A brand manager's job is to make sure customers are thinking the right thing. If a product is better than customers realize, branding can help. You sometimes hear a politician's supporters complain, "If voters really knew him, they'd like him better." That's a politician who needs better branding.

Anyone who has traveled will have noticed tourists in Prague/Nairobi/Beijing heading for McDonald's, despite all the excellent local fare: they are responding to the allure of the known when surrounded by unknowns. Brands reinforce loyalty by using a consistent, recognizable image everywhere the customer is likely to encounter them.

Customers always believe a branded item is worth more than a generic one, even though the two may be similar. On a rational level, we assume that if a large company invests effort and money in building up a brand, it must be good. So we pay $200 for the Sony DVD player even though the prices from makers we haven't heard of start at $50. While the Sony probably is better— more reliable, more features, and so on— is it really four times better? More likely, it's two or three times better, and the remaining price difference can be attributed to Sony's brand worth. Sony, obviously, tries to maximize this effect in order to build its revenues and drive up its share price.

Challenger brands try to steal some of this advantage by imitating the look and feel of Sony packaging to gain part of the trust we feel toward Sony. Sony also inspires its own employees to do better at every stage of the development, manufacturing, and marketing. This internal branding helps it make better products, and gives it a powerful advantage over lesser competitors.

Just having a recognized name and label can raise the perceived quality of an item too. There is some logic to this, as experience tells us there's usually a correlation between the quality of packaging and the quality of what's inside. We're more likely to try a new product by someone we trust, so we look for clues and hints in the packaging: the style of illustration, the typography, and the place of origin.

But we buy brands for reasons that go beyond the rational. Buying a brand is an act of self-affirmation and approval. It gives the customer entry into an imaginary world, built by advertising and publicity, in which aspirations are fulfilled and values reaffirmed. This is why customers often ignore the savings and comparable quality of supermarkets' generic-label goods, and continue to buy big-name brands. They make you feel better. When you buy Heinz beans, you get to be like the person in the TV commercial with the ideal kitchen, the ideal family, the ideal lifestyle… We all know this is a fantasy, but we indulge ourselves. That is the great art and accomplishment of advertising. If you buy generic beans, you save a few pennies, but you get … just beans. No indulgence. No approval of your values. No affirmation that you are part of an ideal world.

A brand manager's job is to create the image that reinforces reputation, encourages loyalty, assures quality, conveys worth, and grants affirmation.

What branding cannot do is rescue a lousy service or salvage a flawed product, especially after a customer has had an unsatisfactory experience with it. Morris Hite, a famous adman, knew that while advertising could pique a customer's curiosity once, an unhappy encounter with reality could rule out a second chance.

The brand has enormous power to enhance the thing it represents, so long as it never loses its connection with the reality of that thing.

Branded identity
These girls at a street festival in New York City after September 11, 2001, demonstrate both their cultural and ethnic identity through their clothing, and their national identity through the flags they hold. All brands make use of conventional symbols to communicate their essential qualities, even when those qualities are complex.

Added value
Electronics made by Sony sell for more than those made by lesser brands. This is partly because the products are better—more innovative, of higher quality and better design—and partly because the brand elicits trust and a sense of extra value.

Staying on message
Advertising sometimes tries to communicate too much at once, distracting audiences from the insights at the heart of the brand. Nearly all cell-phone companies claim to be the "best" or have the "most." Customers never remember which is which. Instead of offering technical claims, brands should try to build an emotional bond with audiences. At the same time, this billboard is trying to communicate a switch in brand identities. What are audiences to understand about the brands?

2006
JAGUAR
X-TYPE

THE JAGUAR OF WAGONS

Throughout its history, Jaguar has made some of the world's most remarkable sports cars and luxury sedans. But until recently, it had never designed an automobile quite like the 2006 X-TYPE Sportwagon. At last, there is a way to combine Jaguar luxury and Jaguar performance with the practicality and security of an all-wheel-drive wagon. The first production wagon ever made by Jaguar, it has been worth the wait. The attention to detail is evident throughout its design.

The X-TYPE Sportwagon gets its versatility from a cargo area that measures a full 50 cubic feet (1413 L) with its 70/30-split rear seats folded down. The space is fully optimized, with very little room taken up by the intrusion of the rear wheel wells, which means you can use the X-TYPE Sportwagon to accommodate the various aspects of your lifestyle. Bright metal scuff strips run across the edge of the cargo floor, and thick, durable carpet covers the cargo surfaces.

Most importantly—the 2006 X-TYPE Sportwagon fulfills your expectations of Jaguar comfort, Jaguar character and Jaguar confidence. Like its X-TYPE sedan counterparts, the X-TYPE Sportwagon gets its powerful acceleration from a smooth, muscular 3.0L V6 engine. And the Sportwagon gets its handling precision from the Jaguar Traction 4 all-wheel-drive system, making it a compelling alternative to ordinary SUVs. When your adventures take you places where snow-covered roads are the norm, the X-TYPE Sportwagon takes you there in style and security.

TECHNOLOGY

To provide for the conflicting demands of driving, Jaguar was the first production car to offer voice activation. Now it adds *Bluetooth*® wireless technology. Available as an accessory and factory-fit option on all X-TYPE models, *Bluetooth* technology lets you connect your X-TYPE to your Jaguar-approved *Bluetooth*-capable phone.

Once connected, your cell phone's contact list and other details can be transferred via *Bluetooth* wireless technology to your X-TYPE, so you can speed-dial from your list of contacts using the X-TYPE's radio keypad. Even if your phone is in a pocket, purse or briefcase, your incoming calls are routed through the car's audio system, with a built-in microphone for hands-free operation. JaguarVoice® provides the X-TYPE driver with access to voice-activated control of the audio, climate control, phone and optional navigation systems- by speaking simple voice commands.

The X-TYPE is available with Reverse Park Control (RPC), a feature that uses ultrasonic sensors embedded in the rear bumper to help ease the task of backing into parking spaces and out of driveways. As you approach an obstacle when backing up, a warning sound emitted with increasing frequency helps you gauge the closing distance between your bumper and the obstacle. The X-TYPE is also available with Jaguar's multi-function Satellite Navigation System. DVD-based, the system serves up street maps in an instant, helping you see where you are going and how to get there.

Feature may not be available on all phones. Please consult with local dealer. *Bluetooth® necessary.* *Standard on Sport Edition and Luxury Edition in Canada.*

Meeting expectations
Customers quickly realized that this car was essentially a rebadged Ford Mondeo, which lacked the quality they expected from Jaguar, and sales lagged. Many auto-industry observers also felt the X-type was dragging down the value of the Jaguar brand on better models, such as the XJ. In comparison, Mercedes and BMW successfully introduced lower-priced cars without damaging their brands because, under the hood, the car was still a Mercedes or a BMW, with the level of quality that customers expected.

Who owns the brand?

"Romulus set the tone for the thousand years that followed. He was decisive. He was extremely dangerous. He liked to build things, and to kill things, too... those are the qualities that made Rome work. In the beginning, Romulus gave the company the one essential gift only a founder can provide: the concept of the corporation."

Stanley Bing, *Rome, Inc.: The Rise and Fall of the First Multinational Corporation*

The real owner of the brand isn't the marketing or communications director. Or the vice president in charge of sales. Certainly not the creative director at the new ad agency who won the account last month. The head of the entire organization (the chairman or the CEO) is the owner of the brand. The brand is intrinsic to the product or service offered, and needs to be supported by all operations. Brand decisions must be taken at the top, and every decision taken at the top should be viewed as a decision about the brand. The brand can't work if it's just a label slapped on as an afterthought, and if the brand doesn't work, the organization won't reach its full potential either.

Until the end of the twentieth century, this was considered a radical idea in business circles. In spite of constant urging by management gurus such as Tom Peters, many companies still aren't organized to reflect the primacy of the brand. Many writers on branding have proposed that it is the customers who own the brand. While this, too, seems radical at first, remember where the brand really resides: in customers' minds. How can customers not own the brand, if it's their neurons that hold onto it?

As we saw in the first chapter, branding is always a two-way process, a dialogue between producers and customers to define a brand's promise in a believable way. Each side plays a different, but vital, role.

A company must listen to its customers. The story of Wrigley's chewing gum is a good illustration of this. William Wrigley started out in the nineteenth century selling soap. As a marketing promotion, he included a sample of baking powder with each box of soap. Soon, he found that the baking powder was more popular than the soap, and switched his business to selling baking powder instead. As a marketing promotion,

Brand values
Ben Cohen and Jerry Greenfield started a homemade ice-cream company in Vermont, in 1978, with just a few hand-mixers for equipment. From the start, their brand's appeal was based on hippie-style wholesomeness; Ben and Jerry's smiling faces on the top of every package were a guarantee of this. As the company grew, Ben and Jerry tried hard to adhere to their entrepreneurial values—fair treatment of workers, the use of natural ingredients, and involvement in local communities. When they sold the company to Unilever in the late 1990s, one of the conditions was that these values be maintained.

he included a small packet of chewing gum… Wrigley gave the people what they wanted, letting customers define his brand, with enormous success.

Sadly, many companies do a rather poor job of listening to their customers. Although many claim to be "customer-centric" and to put the customer's concerns first, large organizations tend to be set in their ways. Too often they are driven by technology, distribution, profit margins, or efficiency, and ignore their customers. These other things are all vital to a firm's health, but they are of no interest to the customer.

If companies want their brands to succeed, they must look at and manage their brands purely from a customer's point of view, even to the extent that they temporarily ignore their self-interest in other areas.

Apple is a company driven by its brands— Macintosh, iPod, and iPhone. Hewlett-Packard, IBM, and Xerox are driven by their technology. Who owns Apple's brand? Steve Jobs, the founder and CEO, together with legions of loyal Mac and iPod fans. Who owns Hewlett-Packard's, IBM's, and Xerox's brands? If that answer were clearer, their brands might be stronger.

The brand development process

"It was a big epiphany that there was a real discipline around this activity. 'Branding' has the general aura of just the creative element, but having a real process allowed us to get beyond personal likes and dislikes."

Karen McCabe, Marketing Manager, IEEE

Many brand consultants' books and websites are filled with diagrams and flowcharts meant to illustrate their unique approach to the brand development process. These circles, squares, arrows, and spirals aim to simplify what is in reality a subtle and flexible process that needs to be tailored to each individual situation.

Some branding experts give their patented methods motivational names or clever acronyms. Others lay out their approach in plain language. Usually, both kinds of explanation boil down to the same thing: analyze a brand's strengths and weaknesses, learn what people love or hate about it, and figure out ways of improving it. Most go about it like this:

Step 1: Research the current situation
Diligent research can bring to bear insights the client was lacking. This step is usually called something like "discovery," because it involves learning what has gone before, and why it has (or hasn't) succeeded.

Step 2: Imagine an ideal future
This involves synthesizing all the ideas and research, and coming up with a key insight about how the brand can transcend its specific product category or customer needs to stand for something greater.

This is often referred to as the "innovation" or "imagination" step. Companies that make innovation a habit usually end up with strong brands. Jennifer Rice, a branding expert at the consultancy Prophet, has drawn a connection between the branding process and the psychologist Abraham Maslow's well-known hierarchy of human needs. Brands that appeal to "higher" needs, such as self-actualization or transcendence, will be seen as more worthwhile than those that simply feed us or make us feel safe.

Step 3: Combine strategy and creativity
A successful brand manager must corral people, business processes, technology, marketing, investment, and all the other areas that might contribute to the outcome, and make the brand happen. This is never simple, and often takes years of hard work (not to mention lots of money). Strategy alone won't succeed; it must be accompanied by a creative identity that engages the senses appropriately, and enough publicity and advertising to arouse demand for the brand.

Step 4: Wait to let it catch on, then do Step 1 again
Design, test, redesign, retest. Of course, research, analysis, and testing are critical, but it is equally critical to read the results correctly. Some products give promising test results but do poorly in the market; other products that nearly died in the research phase have gone on to become accidental hits in the market. It is always important to allow room for customers to discover and adopt an innovation on their own terms.

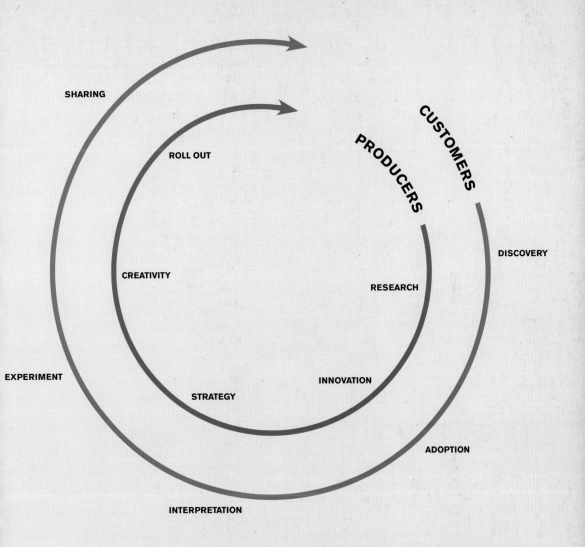

SHARING

ROLL OUT

CUSTOMERS

PRODUCERS

DISCOVERY

CREATIVITY

RESEARCH

EXPERIMENT

INNOVATION

STRATEGY

ADOPTION

INTERPRETATION

Continual brand refinement
The procedures for effective
brand development tend to
be circular, due to the ongoing
dialogue between producers
and customers. Each "rotation"
should result in an identity
that expresses the brand
insight, and fulfills customer
expectations more fully.

Consistency and change

"It is not the strongest of the species that survive, nor the most intelligent, but the ones most responsive to change."

Charles Darwin

Great brands never change, and change constantly. The core of what appeals to a customer—a brand's meaning and values, its promise, and the satisfaction it gives—should be constant, giving customers something to believe in and remain loyal to, over the long term.

The manifestation of a brand—external factors like package design, advertising, and web experience; and internal factors like product design, processes, and flavors—not only can, but must change. Their evolution needs to reflect customers' changing perceptions and expectations, as well as market developments by competing brands.

Paradoxically, it is only by changing that a brand can maintain its constant position in the customer's mind and offer an experience consistent with a customer's own changing self. A strong brand can withstand even radical change in what it sells: Lego used to sell wooden toys, not plastic bricks. Delta Air Lines used to operate crop dusters, not carry passengers. Samsung exported fruit and dried fish. Oracle used to sell mainframe databases, not web-based software.

Colombina packaging makeover
When updating Colombina's packaging (see *before* left and *after* right), designers at Minale Tattersfield carefully redesigned some elements, but retained others to remind customers of the old, familiar design. They also made subtle changes to bring consistency to the packages and give the right visual priority to the brand hierarchy: Colombina (the maker), Pirulito (the product line), and the identities of the individual flavors and varieties (e.g. Dalmatas).

Since customers are constantly changing, and people change from one culture to the next, it is only natural that a brand should look and feel different today from how it did 20 years ago. Any brand should look and feel different in America and in Asia.

The worldwide brand consultancy Interbrand frequently advises its clients that global brands should follow what they call the 70/30 Rule: that 70% of the brand presentation should be constant, and 30% should be adapted to the local culture. This means that for most brands, about one-third of the elements that define it—name, logo, product design, colors, flavors, typography, photographic or illustrative style, local web presence, advertising claims, and so on—

will need some degree of adaptation when the brand crosses borders. Even within a single market, a certain frequency of change is vital. One of the distinguishing features of modern pop culture is its emphasis on the new, and a constant thirst for "the next big thing." Brands that intend to stay relevant need to keep up with constantly shifting trends and tastes in pop culture and adapt swiftly and regularly in line with them in order to avoid being perceived as passé. This isn't to say brands should be as fickle as their customers: the core values, benefits, and attributes must remain constant—only the physical aspects should be updated.

It takes some skill to strike the right balance. Many great brands, from Coca-Cola and Marlboro to IBM and Kodak, have suffered because they misjudged the need for change. They either overshot the mark with ill-conceived changes, or lagged far behind the market and neglected to change.

Evolution vs. revolution

Agencies sometimes offer up incremental changes in identity or package design as a "rebranding," although really they are not rebranding at all. Frequently it isn't the brand's essence—the underlying insights, values, and ideas—that is changing, only the visual presentation. Hopefully, such an update results in an appearance better suited to the existing brand. When this kind of change occurs repeatedly, a brand can evolve quite a different look over time.

This isn't to say the brand itself doesn't also evolve. Less noticeable, but equally important, are changes affecting the brand in other respects: the product functions, the customer support, the strategy for satisfying customer needs, the employees' concept of the brand, and so on. These are just as much a part of the brand as the logo or label, but are much harder to replace overnight. When they are put in place, such "core" changes have a more profound effect on the brand.

GE has changed radically over time, but doesn't have any "revolutionary" moment in its past. The brand has evolved steadily, but subtly. Jack Welch, longtime CEO of GE, was famous for talking about the same thing in every interview—GE values. Meanwhile, IBM—which began with office equipment, switched to computers, and now focuses on business consulting services—has often changed in sudden bursts, as when it sold off its pioneering PC business to Lenovo in 2004. Interestingly, it has kept the same iconic logo throughout its revolutions, a reflection of the fact that the more the brand has changed, the more its fundamental values have remained the same.

A constant idea
The iconic image of a little
girl walking through the rain,
spilling salt behind her, has
graced boxes of Morton Salt
for decades. While the idea is
constant, the actual drawing
has been updated periodically,
as these "revival" packages
show. Morton Salt is a prime
example of how a brand can
add value to what is essentially
a commodity product.

Technological development often forces change, and not just in technology sectors. Change makes yesterday's hot innovations suddenly seem "so five minutes ago," and has a nasty habit of negating competitive advantages literally overnight. Brand benefits that are based only on a technological edge seldom last long. Patents expire, prices drop, and competitors come up with better solutions. When a brand has no appeal beyond the useful benefits of its current form, its days are numbered.

The greatest brands have a meaning that transcends practical benefits. That transcendence allows them to embrace change unafraid, allowing for more consistent customer satisfaction and a longer-lasting brand than competitors who focus only on immediate benefits.

Perception follows image
The old identities for the
Korean conglomerate
Samsung were associated
with low-end products from
a technological laggard. The
new identity, by Lippincott
Mercer, communicated the
added value of a technology
leader, while maintaining
elements that suggested
honesty and longevity—
qualities that were unchanged.
The results were, to some
extent, self-fulfilling.

Design in branding

Design is the process of giving something a deliberate aesthetic form. Design in branding starts with the design of the product, and progresses outward through packaging and labeling to advertising and collateral marketing material such as web pages, brochures, signs, clothing, forms (e.g. bills and invoices), gift items, and anything else that's appropriate to the brand.

Primarily, design concerns the visual and the tactile. Since these are our two most powerful senses, design is probably the single most important tool in branding. Smell, sound, and taste can also be designed, although this is done less frequently.

Designers have a valuable role to play in brand development. Many designers have a finely honed understanding of how people interact with things in their environment. They are well-trained problem solvers who can summon the inspiration needed to cure a brand's ailments. Designers' insights are often crucial to creating brand identities that are meaningful and lasting.

In the world of advertising and branding agencies, some argue that designers should collaborate directly with clients in brand development, while others feel a go-between (such as an account manager) should take on the role of absorbing the client's legal, financial, research, production, logistical, and marketing considerations and interpreting them for designers, leaving the latter free to "be creative." Which approach is best depends on the particular client, case, and designers.

Retro design
The Fiat 500, an icon of mid-century Italian design, is set to enjoy a renaissance similar to that of the Beetle and the Mini. The classic Fiat 500, a symbol of 1960s Italy (left); and its twenty-first-century update (right).

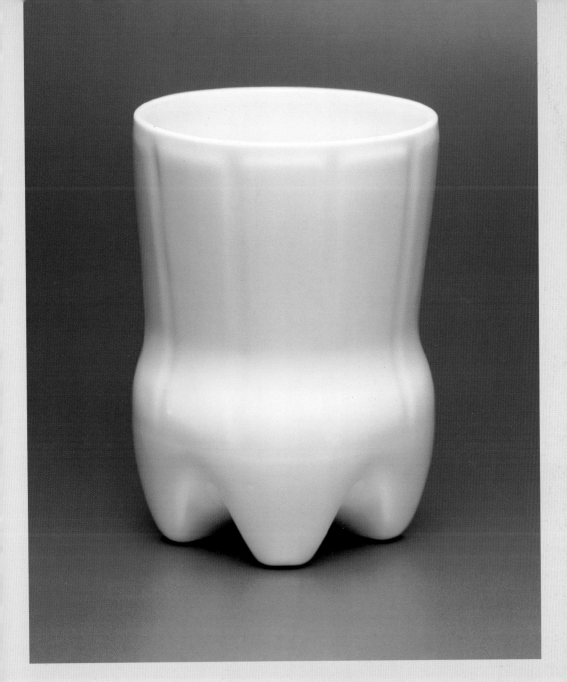

Referencing classic design
A ceramic cup by Qubus Design borrows cleverly from the well-known form of a two-liter plastic Coca-Cola bottle. This object works because the reference is familiar; the cup is at once a riff on a popular shape, and comment on the values of a disposable culture epitomized by brands.

When a great design becomes the icon of an era, the design becomes a brand itself. This has happened with several popular cars. The New Beetle and New Mini are examples of carmakers seeking to capitalize on the brand appeal of a particular model by reviving its design. (Interestingly, the New Mini was produced by BMW rather than its original maker, but BMW smartly made no attempt to link the little car to the BMW brand.)

Package design performs a vital supporting role. Sometimes, as with the BP oilcan, it becomes the product, more often packaging serves as a handy container and store sign saying, "Buy me," but most of all, a package has to tell the customer what to expect: it has to convey the brand promise, not just in words and pictures, but also through the subtle suggestion of shape, function, materials, colors, typeface, and graphics. Design is also a key element of advertising, and of collateral material such as gift items and clothing. A marketing campaign must maintain a visual consistency across all advertising media—web, print, TV, outdoor— while also keeping a clear relationship to the product and its package design (which usually exist prior to the campaign).

Ad designs change more rapidly than product or package designs: each marketing campaign cycle is new and evolves to meet new expectations. This difference in the speeds at which the designs of a brand change can present big challenges to the brand manager, who must keep the brand meaningful and coherent.

Package design

Design development can take a long time. Testing is often done to determine whether the designer's insights and hunches are borne out by contact with real customers in lifelike situations. When Minale Tattersfield were commissioned by BP in the 1980s to design a new plastic oil container, the process lasted six years.

The result was a good example of how a package can be more important than the product. Motor oil is fairly generic. I doubt if customers can tell by examining it whether it's the right one for their car; labeling has to guide them. Motor oil is also rather messy, so a package has to ensure that the customer won't come into contact with the product. With its clever drip-proof, drop-proof, leak-proof, and flameproof design, as well as its strong brand identity, Minale's new BP oil container revolutionized the industry and immediately became the standard. The package had become the product. Most of the other oil companies soon copied it, but BP was ahead of the pack and the brand gained a lasting benefit from being a leader— six years well spent.

Product design

Money is the other thing, besides time, needed to achieve great design. Gillette invested around US $700 million (c. UK £350 million) on researching and developing the Mach3 razor, and hundreds of millions more in marketing it. Worthwhile? The Mach3 was popular and hugely profitable, earning Gillette hundreds of millions in worldwide sales during the years when it was their top-of-the-line razor. Any man who opened a packet of new blades and wondered how a few slivers of steel and plastic could cost so much gained an understanding of the role played by design and branding in product success. The Mach3's appearance, and the way it works, didn't happen by accident: it is a $700-million-dollar razor.

Functional packaging
BP oilcans, designed by Minale Tattersfield. Development and testing lasted six years and established BP as the industry leader.

Packaging aesthetics
Designed by Gillette, with graphic identity and packaging by Interbrand. This new line represented millions of dollars of design work. It's not cheap living up to the brand claim "the best a man can get."

Branding, advertising, public relations, and marketing

"Even in the world of theater, what actors say is less important than what they do. That's why any director will tell you, 'Action is character.' In our world, action is branding."

Bill Schley and Carl Nichols, Jr., *Why Johnny Can't Brand*

The practice of branding is a distillation of activities that were first developed during the nineteenth and twentieth centuries as marketing, advertising, public relations, graphic design (once called commercial art), and corporate identity. These intertwined areas deal with sales, recognition, reputation, customer loyalty, and, last but not least, visual aesthetics. Because these areas all converge on one thing—a brand—and their purpose is to build and promote that brand, they can all be considered aspects of a unified field: branding.

What relationships between branding and these other practices have evolved over the last 20 years? Which should lead the others in the future?

Marketing has traditionally been guided by the "four Ps," being product, place, promotion, and price. In his book *Married to the Brand*, William J. McEwen adds a fifth—people. A company's people need to believe in the brand in order to be able to convey it convincingly to customers. These are the essential elements that every brand manager needs to master in order for a brand to be successful.

Historically, advertising was seen as the leading tool for brand building, but by the start of the twenty-first century, the power of traditional advertising began to decline. While still useful for fashioning an image, telling stories, and maintaining awareness, advertising has limited power to launch a new brand or communicate change in a brand. Thanks to its own ubiquity and intensity, advertising is simply tuned out by large numbers of people and so has difficulty reaching many types of customers.

Many critics of advertising look at how sellers use ad campaigns to control what customers *perceive*, and rightly point to a loss in advertising credibility. But branding fulfills a broader role by trying to control what customers actually *receive*, and by taking into account customers' feedback and definitions of brand meaning.

James Twitchell's book *Twenty Ads that Shook the World* cites numerous examples of advertising's triumphs. These are actually triumphs of branding in which advertising played a leading role.

Public relations (PR) is now a preferred means of getting initial publicity for a new product, handling a crisis, or repositioning a brand. PR agencies use various methods to get the word out, mostly by staging events and feeding stories about a client's offerings to the media, which then carry them to the public. PR firms pride themselves on acting invisibly: their message is more effective if the public thinks it comes from an impartial source, such as the nightly news, rather than from an advertiser.

Graphic design, which has long had a defining voice in brand identity, offers more than the decorative trappings or superficial aesthetics of a brand. By bringing creative thinking to bear in solving challenges; by staying on top of fashions and aesthetic trends; and by integrating left-brain and right-brain insights into one solution, with the benefit of long experience, graphic designers are often better positioned than their counterparts in advertising, PR, or marketing to determine how appearances and perceptions can make a brand relevant and compelling, and to present a real solution to abstract questions.

Forefather of branding
One of the founders of brand identity, Paul Rand, a leading mid-twentieth-century graphic artist, had powerful insights into how design shapes perceptions.

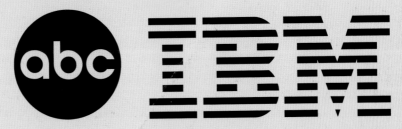

Literal as pictorial
Highly stylized renderings of letters, like these classics by Paul Rand for IBM and ABC, function as pictorial icons.

Storytelling, experience, and emotion

"One of the things Massimo [Vignelli] taught me about designing identities is that it's often easier if you find something that has some history, because it might still have a purchase on people's imagination."

Michael Bierut, Pentagram, interviewed in the *New York Times*, 2007

Every brand needs to tell a story. People love a great story, and the best storytellers have an uncanny ability to forge a personal, emotional bond with their audience. The experience of enjoying a good story is a powerful one that pulls in all of our senses and immerses us so that we feel as if we ourselves are actually living the story.

Many brand practitioners say they focus on branding the experience of using a service or product. Experience is the best way to appreciate something; the experience is usually the most memorable aspect of each thing we buy.

Scott Bedbury, in his book *A New Brand World*, points out a fundamental paradox of branding: as competing products in a category become more alike in their design and basic functions, all that differentiates them is the superficial attributes that are trivial to the object's purpose. These are, in fact, the stories that tie us emotionally to the brand.

When you rent a car, you can be confident that you will know how to drive it, even though you've never sat at the wheel of that make or model in your life. All cars are designed to be familiar; all the controls sit more or less in the same place and work the same way. So what distinguishes one car brand from another? Style, luxury, little extras—things that make little difference to the function of getting from A to B.

Kevin Roberts, the CEO of advertising agency Saatchi & Saatchi, likes to call brands "lovemarks," meaning that the best trademarks appeal to us because we love what they stand for. Few of the decisions we make in life are strictly the result of rationally weighing up the pros and cons. More often—whether or not we are aware of it or admit it—emotions drive our behavior, including our buying.

Making the customer the designer
In a movement called grass-roots marketing by some, companies attempt to involve customers in all phases of the brand, including designing the product and telling the story behind it. Over a year before it rolled out the new

Fiat 500, the Italian carmaker launched a website on which fans of the brand could post home videos showing how their old 500 fit into their lives. The site also gave them the opportunity to use interactive tools to create a personal color and trim scheme for the 500 of their dreams.

GALLERY

500 race

Rear

CentoLew

Rear

Rear

Help | Colours | Sports accessories | **Lifestyle accessories** | Gallery

Remove accessorize

I'd like this one

Characters and personas
One way to give a brand added appeal is to tie it closely to a beloved character from a familiar story, either by paying to license a copyrighted persona, or by adopting a character in the public domain.

An example is Brer Rabbit, the popular folk figure from the American South, used by B&G Foods to sell molasses. In this case, because the product is already associated with Southern culture, the tie-in works.

Bernd Schmidt, one of the first advocates of the concept of "experiential marketing," says all our purchase decisions are essentially made in order to engage in a certain experience. The best brands, according to Schmidt, are those that communicate their promise of a unique experience in a clear and compelling way.

Why does all the "soft stuff"—stories, emotions, and experience—matter? The left half of our brain is the rational half. It adds up facts, compares prices, and dutifully ranks the pros and cons. The right half of our brain is the intuitive half: it desires something because it's fun, because our friends have one, because it'll look terrific. Nowadays, successful brands use every means available to create an emotional, story-based experience: retail environments, web experience, brand ambassadors, word-of-mouth campaigns. These work for the simple reason that they appeal to our right brain.

Spinning a story to accompany the brand offers many marketers an irresistible temptation. In *All Marketers Are Liars*, Seth Godin discusses examples of brand stories stretching into the realms of the odd, the improbable, and the downright mendacious.

Sometimes the culprit is a small detail, almost an afterthought. Since brands with a long tradition seem to generate greater loyalty, many brands pretend they've been around—and loved—for years in their place of origin. Stella Artois was first brewed in 1926, but its label says "Anno 1366" in small letters. Sounds impressive, but in reality, the only thing dating that far back is a deed on a certain house in Leuven, Belgium, which later happened to hold a brewery. There is nothing of Stella Artois that dates back to the fourteenth century.

Likewise, the restaurant chain Red Lobster, which originated in Florida, decided to strengthen its brand by telling customers it originated in Maine, which is well known for its many lobsters. However, there isn't a Red Lobster restaurant within several hundred miles of Maine.

Sometimes, the "lie" is a big one. When Bailey's cream liqueur was created in the early 1970s, its producers fabricated an image of Irish tradition, despite the fact that the product is not from Ireland and had no tradition whatsoever. After the drink caught on, the brand story was refined to give it a sexier appeal.

What each of these and many other brand stories—truthful or not—have in common is that they are credible, and they somehow make the brand more attractive. Customers accept them as part of the bargain: I'll pay more for your brand, and you'll let me take part in a tale.

Brand "history"
What is the meaning of "1366"? What assumptions do customers make when they see this on the label? Are they correct? Many brands attempt to confer a sense of worth through suggesting a long tradition.

Authenticity

"If I could patent 'being real,' I think
I could own that."

Tupac Shakur

To win over increasingly savvy (and jaded) customers, many brands now strive for something generally called "authenticity." They want to be perceived as "real." In other words, they want to be let through the walls and filters that customers put up to guard their private lives from commercial intrusion. Authenticity is also one more way to appear different amid a crowded field of brands that are perceived as superficial and essentially fake. Brands seen as "authentic" elicit a more positive reaction from consumers who feel exploited by mass-market brands and don't want to be seen as following the herd. Authentic brands "matter" in people's lives.

The trend toward authenticity may be related to the popularity of so-called reality television programming, in which nonactors react spontaneously to real-life situations without following a script. It also fits in with the movement toward greater transparency in all media brought about by the Internet, especially the rise of community forums and blogs that encourage constant, open feedback on everything from books and politics to sports teams, celebrity lifestyles, and music.

The quest for authenticity is shaping the travel business, the fashion industry, and many other fields. Travelers choose not just a destination, but a set of activities typical of the place. Fashions aim for "street cred" and try to make a meaningful statement of social awareness. Food and drinks brands, personal-care products, and automobiles likewise try to position themselves as representing an original choice, rather than a response to mass-market advertising.

In the 1990s, one maker of soap powder in the Czech Republic began selling "Regular brand" soap in plain white boxes with simple black type. The box was familiar to millions of television viewers as the unnamed competitor in TV commercials for major brands from P&G and Unilever. "Regular brand" powder sold amazingly well, at least until customers tired of the joke.

Humor is often employed to make a brand seem accessible. It's hard to see how drinking the same bottle of Sprite as millions of others qualifies you as "original," but the advertising does make that claim. In any case, Sprite has tried to position itself as part of an active/youth lifestyle, using humor to tear down pretense and try to appear "cool." Humor is often used to make a brand more human—make it what speakers of Italian or Spanish would call "simpatico."

It is easy for a big brand to co-opt the latest visual hallmarks of authenticity and apply them to mass-market products. The mark of true authenticity is being small-scale, noncommercial, or even handmade. The visual manifestation of this is constantly shifting—too rapidly for most large producers to keep up. In the end, it will not be the visual aspects that indicate authenticity, but the product quality and customer service that small organizations tend to be so much better at providing on a personal level.

Age and authenticity

Some brands maintain an air of authenticity by steadfastly refusing to update their packaging for years or even decades. Others use "retro" revivals of earlier package designs to remind buyers of the brand's longevity, and rely on the power of nostalgia to boost sales.

Unique designs

The Free City Supershop in Malibu, California, sells US $200 (c. UK £100) T-shirts, bicycles, and a seemingly random assortment of other items. It also gives away free orange juice. All of the items are specially designed by artist friends of the owner Nina Garduno. Customers say the brand, which defies easy categorization, feels authentic. Others say that big brands like Gap have been influenced by Free City's style.

Brand discovery

The conventional wisdom in marketing, design, and branding is that *everything* communicates in some way. Brands that give little thought to their communication, the thinking goes, must be communicating badly. How is it, then, that some brands succeed even without any advertising? Why do some brands have loyal fans despite breaking all the rules of good presentation and seemingly doing everything to demolish their own "brand equity"?

"Underground" brands appeal to people precisely because they are not supported by masses of advertising. Buying them seems like a rebellious, individual kind of action. Brands that don't market appear somehow more authentic. Showing them off is a statement that you haven't succumbed to the manipulative advertising that pervades the modern commercial landscape. But of course, this appeal can be exploited by marketers. There are several strategies used by companies to achieve a paradoxical success-by-not-appearing-successful, and they all rely on one thing: the passionate desire of certain customers to "discover" a brand for themselves.

Everyone wants to feel special. Buying the same mass-market brands may provide many kinds of satisfaction, but feeling unique isn't one of them. Everyone wants to feel like part of a community; meaningful communities tend to be small, so buying mass-market products doesn't make us feel part of one.

The late, great Marcello Minale's book *How to Keep Running a Successful Design Company* is a collection of meditations on many aspects of design, architecture, and branding. He cites the example of Dr. Martens boots—universally referred to as "Doc Martens." Doc Martens began life as workingmen's boots, but became adopted as a symbol of authenticity by English mods, skins, punks, and Goths. They crossed the seas, together with English music,

Tribal branding
Dr. Martens made good working-class boots for over a generation. Then punks discovered them. Now they are an icon, trying hard to keep their "authentic" roots and be discovered by a new generation at the same time.

to find passionate followers worldwide. The company now makes a wide array of shoes and boots for men and women (and even occasionally advertises!), but its brand remains true.

Blackspot shoes are even more radical in their opposition to mass-market branding; they have a model called the Unswoosher, an obvious retort to Nike. The shoes are made from organic hemp and recycled tires, by unionized labor in developed countries. They aren't cheap, but they are successful.

The Jones Soda company was started by a Canadian distributor who saw an opportunity to sell drinks with an alternative appeal. Offered mostly in locations that don't sell drinks, such as skate shops, the labels feature personal photos submitted by customers, and the flavors range from common to, well, alternative. Sugar Plum was a limited-edition flavor, offered one Christmas. Visitors to the website vote on proposed new flavors, like Star Fruit. The brand look is deliberately amateur, though the company carefully picks images that match the brand "ethos" and possess a slightly zany, carefree quality that will appeal to the intended customer.

Some brands take the effort to appear underground to an extreme. In the early 2000s, a European maker of underwear for active lifestyles tried to cultivate an alternative image for the company by commissioning graffiti artists to paint its logo on walls, bridges, and highway overpasses. Needless to say, marketing activities ought to remain legal.

Unique alternatives
Jones Soda uses amateur photographs submitted by its customers. Every bottle on the supermarket shelf is different.

The lifetime brand: reality or myth?

Many brands aspire to "catching" a customer for life. Especially for services, it costs far more to acquire a new customer than to keep an existing one: you need to advertise, rent shops, spend time explaining your services, give away free trials, and so on. Once the customer is in, all you really need to do is send out a bill, answer the occasional phone call, and make sure there's an easy way to upgrade when the time comes.

Most advertising is therefore aimed at the all-important 18–35 age group, hoping that, once "hooked," they'll be retained for life. It's also believed that since everyone aspires to a more youthful identity, any advertisement featuring young people will also appeal to older generations (but not the other way around).

Customers' wants and needs change as they grow older; brands try to provide a range of offerings with appeal to young, middle-aged, and older customers. For example, telecommunications companies try to package their services to appeal to a full range of ages and lifestyles, with different combinations of phones and service plans meant for teenagers, twenty-somethings, thirty-somethings, and older users. They know younger customers will be attracted to, for example, prepaid cards with the hippest new phone and extras like downloads and ring tones, while older customers will demand simpler plans at lower cost, and phones that simply make phone calls. The hope is that as each user matures, he or she will naturally move up to the next appropriate offering, but stay with the same brand. Personal-care brands try to do the same thing. For example, a line of skin cream will have products tailored to teenagers, adult women, and older women. All need different products, so why do they all need the same brand?

Realistically, can lifetime brand loyalty be achieved under a single brand concept? While it makes sense to try and gain a customer for life on a rational, economic level, it is hard to see how a single brand can be interesting to both young and old, energetic and retiring. Teenagers don't want to use the same brands as their parents. People in their forties probably feel they've outgrown the brands they used 20 years ago. Given the rapid pace of change today, it is unlikely that many brands will live as long as their average customer anyway.

Brands that appeal to all ages do so with a single concept that is so simple, it is universal. Coca-Cola, Band-Aid, and the BBC are examples of this: everyone can relate to them. As soon as a company introduces diverse ideas aimed at diverse age groups, it should consider building a discrete brand for each, one capable of focus and strength among its particular users, rather than trying to be all things to all customers.

One way to do this is to invent a new category. When Curad wanted to challenge Band-Aid's near-total dominance of the sticking-plaster category, they introduced decorative plasters for children, in effect creating a new category for their own brand while cutting into Band-Aid's sales.

Brand identities

An organization with a very broad customer base and many products to offer to different audiences faces special challenges in crafting and presenting its brand identity. Appealing to everyone makes it very difficult to keep a brand focused on a clear message. Starting with a fundamentally simple logo and typographic style, the BBC overcomes this challenge by using images crafted to lend sophistication, drama, or humor, as appropriate to the specific communication.

Brand extensions, associations, and co-branding

"The basic approach of positioning is not to create something new and different, but to manipulate what's already in the mind, to retie the connections that already exist."

Al Ries and Jack Trout, *Positioning: The Battle for Your Mind*

The strongest brands occupy a clearly defined and well-focused position in customers' minds. They dominate their categories: Adidas in sportswear, Honda in cars, and so on. But brands often aren't limited to a single category. Adidas sells fragrance. Honda makes motorcycles, boats, and planes. And some überbrands seem to cover everything—GE offers lightbulbs, dishwashers, industrial turbines ... and financial services. Do brands have any limits?

Brands inhabit categories, but are not really *of* those categories. A great brand transcends categorization to stand for a larger, abstract meaning. Adidas is about winning more than sportswear. Honda is about getting around reliably rather than wheels. GE wraps all its offerings in values such as caring and quality.

A great brand can be applied to any category in which it finds its larger truth reflected. Virgin's brand is about exuberance and defiance of the establishment. It works as an icon brand in areas as diverse as music, airlines, and cell phones. (But it didn't work in cola, because nobody ever really felt a need to defy Coke or Pepsi.)

It is important to distinguish between brand extensions, line extensions, and licensed merchandise. Each works for a different reason. Brand extensions can be thought of as functioning vertically: the same brand is used in a new category where the brand's meaning still makes sense to customers. Line extensions tend to be horizontal: they may be geared to higher or lower segments, but they still function broadly within the same category. Licensed merchandise takes the brand and applies it to an item (usually unrelated) made by another firm, to ride on the popularity of the original brand experience.

A brand extension is often accomplished with a sub-brand. Honda's SUVs (sport utility vehicles) include Pilot and CR-V; its coupés, Accord and Civic; its minivans, Odyssey; trucks, Ridgeline; sports cars, S2000; and so on, to bikes, boats, and planes. All carry the Honda brand, which is not narrowly associated with any single category. Companies often try to profit by applying successful brands to new items within the same category or line, like flavors of ice cream. However, this can backfire. When Miller introduced new beer varieties (Miller Lite, Miller Genuine Draft) the aim was to exploit its Miller High Life brand equity in order to appeal to different groups of drinkers. However, by treating the different beers as line extensions, rather than their own brands, Miller diluted the strength of its overall brand.

In the best of cases, brand extension provides "coattails" that help launch a new product. Apple Computer rolled out the iPod music player this way. The Apple brand is about innovation and ease of use, so it works for portable music players as well as computers. Later, the iPod's success provided a "halo" effect that encouraged satisfied users to try using a Macintosh computer for the first time.

Below: Selling adventure
Let's count the brand identifiers on this box: Kellogg's, Disney's, *Pirates of the Caribbean, Dead Man's Chest*, Jack Sparrow, Johnny Depp. I doubt anyone buys this because they enjoy the cereal. Rather, it offers a chance to relive the film's excitement at breakfast.

Above: Relevant extensions
Some brand extensions make more sense than others. This pancake syrup claims to contain a small amount of Jim Beam bourbon as one of its ingredients. Could it be the perfect thing to chase a hangover, or is it just another gimmick to leverage a popular brand in a new category?

Right: Adopting celebrity personas
More than a celebrity endorsement, this low-calorie, half iced tea, half lemonade drink actually takes on the celebrity persona as its brand. The can is covered with photos of the famous golfer, Arnold Palmer, at various great moments in his career.

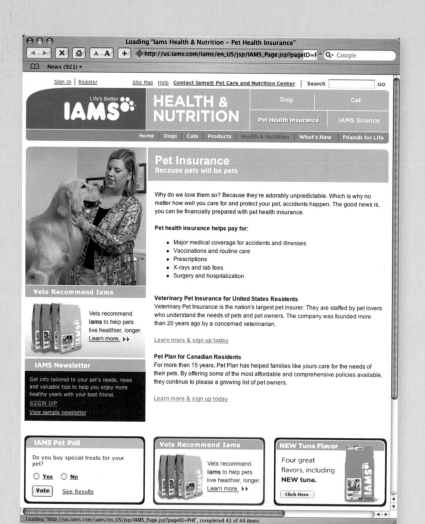

Focused brand extensions
A TippingSprung Brand-
Extension Survey named
Iams pet insurance the
overall winner. "More and
more marketers are looking
at brand extensions as a way
of leveraging the value of their
core brand assets," said one
of the survey's authors.

The limits of customer credulity are often tested in licensed merchandising. Many brands fail when they license their brands in new areas because customers don't believe the brand has any relevance there. Harley-Davidson symbolizes an American lifestyle—rebellion and the freedom of the open road. Its brand is licensed to footwear and men's aftershave, which has some connection, but also to a cake-decorating kit!

In the short term, extensions and merchandise make money, build hype, and give customers a way to "live the brand." Longer term, they may be detrimental, leading to overexposure and loss of focus, hurting sales and market share. One solution is to offer limited-edition or seasonal extensions. The other is to simply refrain from extending the brand, no matter how tempting the short-term gains, if the long-term perspective is questionable.

One of the most effective strategies for a new or growing brand is to associate itself with another, established brand that already has credibility with the audience the new brand is seeking. Such co-branding associations are often analogous to the "four Ps" of marketing (see page 26). Usually, they don't fit squarely into a single category, but straddle two or more.

A **product partnership** works when both brands' offerings have complementary benefits. By joining up, the two can give the customer a package that neither could deliver separately—and, hopefully, that no competitor can offer. The benefit to each is that the audience perception of it is improved through its association with the other. For example, the branding partnerships Intel forged with many computer makers for the "Intel Inside" campaign demonstrate this so-called virtuous circle: Dell, IBM, Gateway, and others were able to show they used the leading microprocessors, while Intel was able to increase the perception of itself as the leader. Likewise, the inclusion of Google's search and advertising features on many other websites allows those sites to offer powerful, integrated features with a mark of familiarity, and also allows Google (in addition to giving it omnipresence) to gather yet more useful data about web users' patterns of behavior.

A **place partnership** allows one brand to piggyback on the distribution of another in order to reach vast numbers of potential new customers. At the same time, the presence of the new brand in the distribution network brings in fresh, enthusiastic customers for the distributor brand. One example of this was the partnership between Starbucks coffee and United Airlines, which came at a time when Starbucks was still expanding and United had a sorry reputation for serving the worst coffee of any airline. Another example would be the link-up between parcel shippers FedEx and the Kinko's chain of copier stores. Copying documents and shipping them was a natural combination for customers; FedEx acquired a large network of storefront locations, while Kinko's acquired new business from firms that were accustomed to using FedEx.

A **price promotion** or partnership will "bundle" two brands into one package, usually at a discount. The idea is that a customer probably wants one or other of the items, and will enthusiastically take both at the combined price. This tactic is usually used when one company owns both brands, for example when Procter & Gamble offer their Crest toothpaste together with their Oral-B toothbrushes. Alternatively, a sample or gift of one product is included free with the purchase of another.

People partnerships are extremely hard to pull off. "People brands" are, by definition, service brands whose key assets—people—have been trained to represent Brand A, not Brand B. The company culture of Brand A is often incompatible with that of Brand B. Such partnerships tend to happen only by necessity, such as after a corporate merger. When Compaq, the personal computer maker, and Digital Equipment Corp., a maker of mainframes, became one, the sales teams of both firms tried to work together under the Compaq brand. It proved to be something of a disaster. The Compaq brand meant little to mainframe customers, while the Digital sales and service people felt like fish out of water in the personal computer business. Both brands, which had been leaders to begin with, lost out.

With considerable foresight, Herb Kelleher, the chairman of Southwest Airlines, once turned down the bargain acquisition of a shuttle airline that was up for sale in the eastern US. As Jack Trout recounts in *Big Brands, Big Trouble*, Kelleher said, "I sure would like their gates in New York, Washington, and Boston. But what I don't want is their airplanes, and more importantly their people."

Co-branding is sometimes used in a quixotic effort to switch customers from an old to a new brand. Cell-phone giants like Vodafone, Orange, and T-Mobile have repeatedly acquired local networks in other countries and rebranded them with their global brand. A transitional period, when the old and new brands are used side by side, allows customers to become aware of the switch. However, since the brand change is most often motivated by corporate acquisitions rather than any fundamental marketing strategy, it is unclear how much goodwill is really transferred from the old brand to the new—or whether such a transfer is even a priority of the new brand owner.

Co-brand teamwork
By teaming up, brands can offer customers a combined package with benefits that neither could offer separately. Apple and Nike joined up to give customers a product that was greater than the sum of its parts—a device that slips into a running shoe and gives the user information about their workout on the display of their iPod.

What else can be branded?

"You don't have to ask the beans in the can how they feel about the label... Brands that involve whole populations need popular permission."

Wolff Olins, Agency brochure for Øresund region branding

The world changed rather dramatically toward the end of the twentieth century. The end of Soviet communism; the advent of the World Wide Web; an economic boom across Asia; the unification of Europe; investment in fiber-optic and wireless networks; the success of big-box retailers like Tesco and Wal-Mart; protests against economic globalization; AIDS; the events of September 11, 2001; and wars in Kosovo, Afghanistan, and Iraq point to how change— on a global scale—has come to the consumer lifestyle and commercial culture of the world's citizens.

During this period, people began applying the term *brand*—previously reserved for soups and soaps—to just about everything: corporate reputations, football players, tourist destinations, and even churches. This probably resulted from the convergence of several trends. First, people began questioning the purpose of marketing in a society oversaturated with commercial messages. The desire to cut away the noise associated with advertising, together with an explosion in the variety of goods and services produced, led marketers to try and pinpoint the simple things that make us buy A instead of B.

Second, large American firms, adjusting to the end of the postwar boom, looked at their competitiveness against international challengers and started to obsess about things like *quality, excellence,* and *innovation.*

Brand ideals
The Olympic rings are among the most recognized and enduring brand identities in the world. Every two years, a new sub-brand is created for each Summer or Winter Games. The International Olympic Committee has to guard carefully against the misuse of the five-ring logo and ensure that the many sponsors of the games use the endorsement in accordance with strict guidelines which guarantee that the identity continues to reflect the ideals and values of the Olympic brand. Haier, a leading Chinese maker of electronics and appliances, is one sponsor of the Beijing 2008 Summer Olympic Games.

Meanwhile their counterparts in Europe, facing a wave of privatization and new competition from the East, began to focus on their image as never before.

Third, the spread of desktop computers meant graphic design became both cheaper and more fun. A small firm could produce work on a par with a big firm.

Finally, the rise of the Internet forced markets to become efficient and transparent. Competition was suddenly just a click away. It didn't take long to realize that elements of soap branding could be—had to be—applied to corporations and destinations too.

A product is fairly easy to brand. Modern manufacturing makes it simple to ensure that the brand promise is kept—satisfaction guaranteed! Every can of Campbell's soup is of the same quality; the label makes that promise and the customer can focus instead on personal issues such as, "Will I like this flavor?" or "Does this contain too much salt?" or "What will my family say if I buy this?" A simple image or story can be repeated ad infinitum.

A service is harder to brand, because it involves interactions between humans, who are changeable. Big service brands tend to overpromise; customers can be left feeling unsatisfied. Since a steady relationship is vital, service companies have to work very hard on training to make sure employees understand *they* are the brand.

Organizations offer their own unique challenges. A university, church, museum, corporation, or nonprofit organization can have a strong brand only if it has strong leadership with a clear and compelling vision.

Places—neighborhoods, cities, regions, nations—acquire their brands organically, the result of thousands or millions of people visiting and forming their own impressions. Changing a country's brand image requires leadership and political skills as well as the coordinated effort of many entities.

People can rebrand themselves at will. Madonna has made a career of it. That's good news for anyone who feels under-appreciated or misunderstood—but you must convince your family and friends (your biggest fans) that you really mean it!

Place branding
With globalization now an established facet of twenty-first-century life, places around the world must compete with each other for the business and tourist dollar. Place branding creates value for a city, region, or country, helping it to attract a share of the world's wealth, talent, and attention. Both Madrid (top) and Manchester (above) have a strong presence internationally, strengthened through the successful branding of their respective soccer teams.

Brand interaction
David Beckham is a brand unto himself. So are Real Madrid and Manchester United. So are the cities those teams belong to. How does Beckham's personal brand interplay with their brands and with the brands he is paid to endorse, such as Gillette? And how will his brand influence perceptions of LA Galaxy, and of soccer in the USA?

Women and men

Vive la différence! Since women and men are so wonderfully different, it's no wonder that many brands try to address them in different ways. Where many brands fall down, however, is in stereotyping their audiences and forcing people into unwanted gender roles. In the past, marketing has often been aimed either at men, or at men's idea of women. Until the 1990s, little brand communication was aimed at women on their own terms.

A general movement toward equality between the sexes, together with greater self-assertion by women in marketing and media, means that now, fewer of Western society's commercial monologues (the media and advertising) are dominated by a male-oriented worldview. More companies have realized that women make buying decisions and wish to be addressed in ways that are not male-defined.

Automobiles, for example, were traditionally sold to men, until numerous studies made undeniable the fact that, not only do many women buy cars themselves, but in many families and couples in which the man buys the car, he listens to his wife's or partner's opinion. Once carmakers accepted this, they began to make changes, both to cars themselves (with changes such as a fold-down makeup mirror on the driver's side as well as the passenger side), and by targeting some of their advertising at women.

Much advertising still addresses and portrays women and men differently, in ways that reinforce their self-positioning through stereotypes. These stereotypes are not always presented in an obvious way: the subtlety of branding for men vs women is often intriguing.

Gender differences
Clinique, a well-regarded women's cosmetics brand, extended itself with a line of men's products during the 1990s. The brand image was subtly restyled for the male audience using different naming—for example, Skin Supplies for Men as opposed to gentler-sounding, gender-unspecified names such as Foaming Cleanser; a different palette (more gray and fewer pastel shades); black-and-white as opposed to color photography; and more informational packaging. The aim was to reassure men that it's OK to buy cosmetics.

dove is pro·age,™
not anti-age.

Redefining beauty
The Dove Campaign for Real Beauty began, in 2005, with an important message for women and girls—normal is beautiful. By addressing issues of self-esteem and self-image, the Dove brand was able to make a compelling pitch to women who feel excluded by conventional images of beauty in the media and advertising—that is, the majority of women. A follow-up campaign, like this video at the Dove website, also addressed issues of ageism in the media.

What do you think?

Click a choice to see your vote count — instantly.

☐ wrinkled?
☐ wonderful?

>>>>>|

Happily, the best brands are able to move past stereotypes of gender (and race and class) to speak to customers as intelligent individuals. Not only "old male" brands for things like cars, but also traditionally "feminine" brands such as Dove soap have discovered that cultivating a passionate following among women involves addressing women in ways that are respectful, joyful, and supportive—in short, sisterly rather than paternalistic. And while this may seem obvious, it was still a courageous step for many brands to take.

One motivation behind more female-oriented branding could be the general trend toward building whole brand experiences. There is empirical evidence that women tend to prefer holistic experiences that engage them on an emotional as well as a rational level. By focusing on experiences, marketers may, intentionally or not, be giving brands greater appeal for women.

Marketers still generally treat men and women as different audiences who respond to different stimuli and different emotional appeals. However, the most interesting and persuasive brands are often the ones that challenge preconceived gender roles rather than repeating them.

Globalization

"People used to worry that the global would destroy the local, but in fact, the global helps the local to untrap itself."

John Tuomey, Irish architect,
The New York Times, January 6, 2006

Brands generally arise in situations of plentiful production. In the US, there were boom periods for new brands after the Civil War in the 1860s and again after WWII. Manufacturers with extra capacity introduced brands as a way to encourage consumption, and as a result of competition with other producers seeking a larger share of a saturated market. Today, established brands come mostly from developed (Western) economies, though it seems only a matter of time before developing nations catch up and begin to see their own brands achieve success, regionally and globally.

The process of catching up is often uneven and unfair. Makers of established brands have an obvious advantage when entering a new or emerging market. They have the know-how and resources to market their brands, and can easily dominate local competition, either by importing or by making their branded goods locally.

Although producing locally creates jobs as well as providing know-how for local managers and workers, multinationals can drive valued and traditional local brands out of business simply because these lack the capital and aggressive management to defend their market. Governments, driven by politics rather than love of brands, don't help much. They tend to look after the jobs and revenues of the big deals, and let small owners of local brands languish.

A global brand can be attractive in a small country simply because of its worldly cachet. Giant makers of fast-moving consumer goods (FMCGs) such as Altria (formerly Philip Morris), Procter & Gamble, Nestlé, and Unilever, capitalize on the efficiency of being very big and simply deploy the same brands and advertising from country to country—even when the products aren't the same. It's no secret, for example, that Stella Artois is brewed locally in places like Croatia and New Zealand, not imported from Belgium; Procter & Gamble customers complained for years that the Tide detergent manufactured in Belgium for Western Europe was of higher quality than the Tide made in the Czech Republic for sale in the East.

Sometimes an enlightened multinational will maintain or revitalize a local brand, perhaps years after it was last seen on the market. In eastern Europe, many local brands were given new life after the end of communism opened the region to foreign investment. Czech carmaker Škoda, long the butt of jokes in countries such as the UK, completely re-engineered its vehicles after Volkswagen took over in 1991. Model names from the 1940s and 1950s, like Felicia and Octavia, were revived and Škoda now regularly wins Car of the Year awards all over Europe. Major breweries in Prague and Pilsen, with only minor upgrades to their products, saw global exports skyrocket to unprecedented levels after new management from SABMiller and Bass took over the brand marketing.

Standing out from the crowd

A familiar brand stands out in the midst of the visual anarchy of generic signage. In these images, the most prominent brands are Western and the generic signs are Asian, but the day will come when that situation is reversed.

Tapping an old source

Until the fall of communism, beer from Pilsen was hard to get outside of Czechoslovakia and the Eastern Bloc. In 1999 it was acquired by the multi-national brewer SABMiller. Thanks to improved brand management, including sales, marketing, and distribution, Pilsner Urquell can now be enjoyed worldwide.

What brands can do for beer or cars, they can do for candy too. Prague's big chocolate maker, Čokoládovny, was acquired by Nestlé and Danone in 1991. Old product brands were livened up and new ones reintroduced to the local market with great success. In one case, the popular, unofficial name of an old favorite—fidorka—was adopted as the new brand name, an excellent example of listening to your customers.

Success doesn't just come when foreigners take over. The maker of Kofola, a Czech soft drink, disappeared after the end of communism, but the brand was brought back in the late 1990s by a group of local managers who had gained experience in marketing for multinationals and started a new venture to revive the once-popular cola.

Globalization seems unstoppable, but many corporations have realized that big, global brands don't enjoy unlimited appeal. There is value in local brands for the simple reason that they form part of the local culture and win over loyal, local customers because they're "ours." But the best local brands can also transcend their borders and go global themselves. China seems to epitomize the next phase of globalization: it is moving away from making commodity goods to building its own brands in shoes, computers, electronics, white goods, and other areas. Interbrand, in its report *Best Brands in China 2006* (produced together with *BusinessWeek*), noted that "among the best Chinese brands, brand management is already relatively sophisticated and progressing at a rapid pace. Chinese brands are increasingly using global best practices and are becoming formidable competitors to non-Chinese brands, both domestically and globally."

Brand revival
Local brands may languish under pressure from global brands, but with skillful management they can be brought back to life, exploiting the goodwill that previously existed in people's minds. Fidorka chocolate wafers, from the Czech Republic, is an example of this.

Market adaptation
Coca-Cola has been developing its global markets for decades. This sign from China dates back to the 1930s. In countries like Thailand, the adaptation of the brand includes flavors that are particular to that market, such as mango-flavored Fanta.

From local to global
One country that has succeeded in taking local brands global in recent years is the Czech Republic. Škoda cars, once the butt of jokes in other countries, are now highly regarded for their engineering, reliability, and stylishness.

Trademark protection and intellectual property

A brand consists of a single insight or idea in the customer's mind, wedded to a sign—a name and symbol—that serves as a convenient shorthand for that idea.

Trouble may arise if two or more ideas (products or services) share the same name or symbol. Apple Computer was sued in the early 1980s for using the same name as the Beatles' record company. The suit ended with an agreement that the computer firm would stay out of the music business.

This is a common sort of arrangement. There is no problem with the same name (or a similar logo) being used by companies that operate in completely different categories or geographic areas: customers are not likely to be confused. However, disagreements can arise when the boundaries blur, as when Apple started selling songs through its online iTunes service, or when the American Budweiser beer tried to move into European markets claimed by the Czech Budweiser, resulting in protracted legal disputes.

A strong brand is the most powerful means for fending off competitors when other tactics such as copyright protection or exclusive distribution are exhausted. When LEGO invented its interlocking plastic bricks in the 1940s, it was able to patent them. But patents eventually expire. LEGO now fends off makers such as Mega Bloks and others by virtue of having a stronger brand, using a combination of design, innovation, quality, and brand experience to maintain the loyalty and passion of its customers.

Trouble of another sort crops up when a name that has long been associated with one company's product becomes a generic term for a whole class of goods. English is littered with words that used to be trademarks: linoleum, cornflakes, aspirin, and dozens more. This happens in other languages too: in Italian, a bus is often called a *pulman* after the old coach maker, Pullman; in Czech, a razor blade is referred to as a *žiletka*, a Slavicized version of the name Gillette. When a name is judged to have become generic, its former owners lose the protection of trademark, since language belongs to everybody and no one can lay claim to a particular word.

This is a cruel irony of successful branding. On the one hand, you want customers to have your name on the tip of their tongue when they articulate a desire for your type of product. On the other hand, the name must be associated not so much with the thing itself (or the product category) as with the quality that transcends it—the insight that raises your product above the other commodity products in the same category.

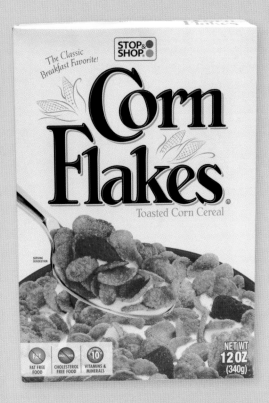

Protecting a brand name
Companies whose brand names are in danger of becoming generic often go out of their way to remind customers that they are still trademarks. Modern legal standards hold that brand names must be unusual and distinct from everyday use in order to be protected as trademarks. Some former trademark names are now generic product names that can be used by anybody, either because they were not adequately defended from copycats or because they were not sufficiently distinctive to begin with.

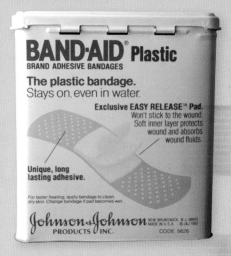

Some trademarks are still acknowledged as belonging to one company, but are so widely used that their owners must be constantly vigilant, lest the names become generic. That's why brands like Kleenex and Band-Aid add the word "brand" in tiny letters under the name on their packaging.

"Let me Xerox that for you." "Please FedEx that to me." "Go ahead and Google it." Each of these actions might just as easily be fulfilled using the services of Canon, DHL, or Yahoo!, respectively. The challenge for brands that risk becoming verbs is not to occupy the number one position in customers' minds—they have achieved that—but to keep customers mindful of why the brand means more than the product. They must achieve a higher insight that transcends product and stands for something more universally appealing. To survive into the future, Xerox needs to be more than just "number one in copiers," FedEx needs to be more than just "overnight," and Google needs to be more than just "search and find."

Brand valuation

"If this business were split up, I would give you the land and bricks and mortar, and I would take the brands and trademarks, and I would fare better than you."

John Stuart, former CEO of Quaker Oats

Brand valuation is controversial. Putting a precise financial value on such a great intangible is impossible, although there are plenty of brand experts who are prepared to make an estimate, and plenty of corporate leaders who take the results very seriously. On the one hand, how can a lawyer put a dollar figure on his reputation? Why do some companies "retire" popular brands if they are worth money? Can we measure precisely how much customers "love" Honda more, or less, than Toyota? On the other hand, it could be argued that the respected law firm is able to charge higher fees because of its good name. Campbell's soup sells for more than the generic brand, representing a return on the brand for every can sold.

Basically, formal methods of brand valuation try to separate the abstract "thing" that is a brand from the more concrete assets whose value is easily measurable in a company, including factories, equipment, and know-how such as patents. The different approaches to brand valuation, and the accounting rules in various countries that allow for recording brand value as an item in a company's financial statements, have the same aim: to provide tools for businesses to plan investments, evaluate mergers and acquisitions, explain the terms of a joint venture, or sue each other for damages.

Each year the global consultancy Interbrand teams up with *BusinessWeek* magazine to rank the world's most valuable brands. They consider only brands of public companies, whose financial results are published, and whose financial performance can be easily separated from the rest of the company's activities. The value of a brand is the market capitalization of the company—the value of its stock—minus hard assets like factories. This shows how much money the brand is earning for its owners.

Young & Rubicam, the worldwide ad agency, takes a different approach with its Y&R Brand Asset Valuator, which it uses as a tool for determining the relative strength of any given brand. It focuses less on economics than on qualitative data, surveying thousands of customers to establish four measures—

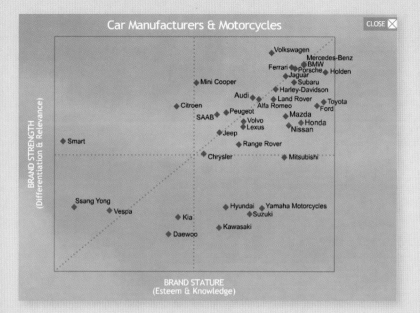

Car Manufacturers & Motorcycles

CLOSE ✕

BRAND STRENGTH
(Differentiation & Relevance)

BRAND STATURE
(Esteem & Knowledge)

- Volkswagen
- Mercedes-Benz
- Ferrari
- BMW
- Porsche
- Holden
- Jaguar
- Mini Cooper
- Subaru
- Harley-Davidson
- Audi
- Land Rover
- Toyota
- Citroen
- Alfa Romeo
- Ford
- Peugeot
- Mazda
- SAAB
- Volvo
- Honda
- Lexus
- Nissan
- Jeep
- Range Rover
- Smart
- Chrysler
- Mitsubishi
- Ssang Yong
- Vespa
- Hyundai
- Yamaha Motorcycles
- Suzuki
- Kia
- Kawasaki
- Daewoo

Left: Brand value
Calculations of brand value based on market capitalization are of more interest to corporate finance executives than to customers. Young & Rubicam's Brand Asset Valuator, on the other hand, assesses how customers view brands qualitatively–that is, how much they like them.

Far left: Perceived worth
Quaker Oats is an old and well-loved brand that also happens to be worth a lot. The brand's popularity allows the product to sell for much more than a generic version.

differentiation, relevance, esteem, and knowledge—with which to plot a brand's relative position in its sector or category.

Each approach has its merits. Two brands might have a clear economic relationship, but might engender very different feelings among customers and inspire different behavior or loyalty. For example, Microsoft's brand always rates well in financial terms because of strong sales, but Apple, although it rates lower in financial terms, is widely seen as a better-loved brand.

Brands represent a dialog, or struggle, between two parties: the producer and the customer. Putting a value on a brand is a bit like betting on a football match: you know how the players have been doing lately, but you still can't be sure who'll win tomorrow. Brands that evoke the greatest passion and

loyalty are often small brands belonging to small companies. Well-loved brands seldom belong to really big companies, so financial valuations inevitably create a paradox, rewarding size while discounting passion. In any case, putting a number on a brand's past performance tells companies little about what they should do in the coming years in order to nurture, expand, rejuvenate, or refocus their brands.

Causes and advocacy

When brands take a stand, who benefits? Why do some companies support charities loudly, while others are more discreet?

The cynical observer will quickly bring down any effort by a big-brand corporation to support a worthy cause, whether it's fighting disease, helping the poor, or protecting the environment. The cynic says it's all a PR gimmick to hide a guilty conscience or a questionable record.

There is no doubt that corporate support for worthy causes does benefit the needier elements of society; it provides billions in funding and countless hours of donated employee time annually. And arguably, the corporations do benefit from the additional goodwill that the publicity surrounding their giving brings.

Customers, too, benefit—if indirectly. As well as making a better society, brands that advocate a good cause show that their parent companies are healthy enough and well-managed enough to be able to spare a thought for "doing good," and well-managed, profitable manufacturers naturally produce better goods and services.

The "green" brand
Established in the 1980s, The Body Shop was one of the first brands to show that concern for the environment or animal welfare could propel a brand to success. Its many imitators only proved how profound and lasting was customers' desire for "advocacy" brands.

Wal-Mart, the largest retailer in the US if not the entire world, decided to "go green" partly as a defensive measure against detractors who claimed the firm was unconcerned with health or the environment. Along the way, Wal-Mart discovered that stocking organic foods was a smart brand initiative. Besides taking the teeth out of detractors' arguments, it put the entire grocery industry in North America on notice that organic and healthy foods belong firmly in the mainstream. This has encouraged more wholesalers to certify their products as organic, grown the entire organic food industry, and resulted in wider distribution and lower prices for all organic foods. The benefits extend far beyond Wal-Mart's own aisles.

Right and bottom:
Environmental conscience
BP's green, white, and yellow
logo was designed to show
the company's commitment
to the environment and solar
power. More than aesthetics,
the campaign included new
sites designed to be partly
powered by energy from the
sun, with solar panels forming
a transparent canopy above
the pumps.

When it comes to <mark>green matters</mark> we develop grey matter.

Our investment in environmental and science
education has helped inspire British school
children for 37 years. In the past 12 months,
teachers in over 2,400 UK schools have chosen
to use our resource packs, which help teach
children about energy issues.

bp

beyond petroleum®

© 2006 BP p.l.c.

bp.com

Left: Organic foods
When Wal-Mart decided that
offering more organic food
would help modernize its
image and broaden its appeal
to urban and other upscale
consumers, the chain asked
its large suppliers to help.
This prompted mainstream
brands to develop organic
versions of their best-selling
food products.

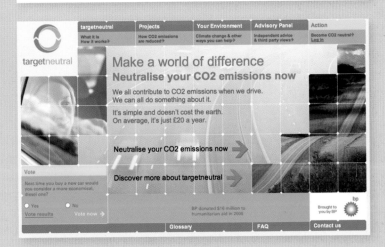

The "justice" brand

Long gone are the days when corporate barons hadn't the slightest concern for workers' well-being. Companies still need to produce their goods as quickly and cheaply as possible, and will often outsource production to regions with less stringent controls on working conditions. Nonetheless, big brands like Nike, Benetton, and Gap are highly sensitive to accusations of using sweatshop labor. All of them have learned, to their cost, that customers expect workers to be treated fairly, and that espousing better treatment is good for their brands.

Giving coffee growers in developing nations a fair price for their harvest—the principle of Fairtrade—is strongly espoused by the Starbucks coffee brand, and other food and drinks brands that want to attract young customers with sophisticated ideas about the world. Starbucks goes so far as to claim that there aren't enough Fairtrade-certified beans for them to buy, and is taking steps to help farmers obtain certification. EDUN, a firm started by Bono and his wife Ali Hewson, sells clothing made in developing countries with the aim of letting those makers retain a larger share of the sale price.

INSPI(RED)

INC(RED)IBLE

Loyalty to brand causes
Brands that embrace a cause can not only do real good in the world, they can also quickly build a loyal and passionate base of customers who share their values.

An excellent and innovative example of brands using their power for good is the (PRODUCT) RED initiative to help fight AIDS in Africa. This brand is unusual in being applied as a co-brand with other major brands—including Gap, iPod, Armani, Converse, Motorola, and American Express—across a range of categories. Aside from helping a good cause, the brands aren't shy about profiting from sales of (RED) products. They benefit from association with the cause, but the cause also benefits from their endorsement.

The "are we OK?" brand

Dove, originally a brand of soap, extended into underwear and other feminine products. The extension worked because the brand's meaning transcended the product category to stand for "inner beauty." To convince women that the brand cared about them, and not just their appearance, Dove started the Real Beauty campaign to communicate to young girls the value of confidence, self-esteem, and a healthy, realistic body image. This included educational television spots, and web discussion forums.

Power of the consumer

We've seen what producers do in their struggle to define the meaning and promise of the brand relationship. But what can customers do? Do brands rule consumers, or vice versa?

A customer's first option is apathy. "Just ignore it." Sellers have to expend a lot of energy to grab buyers' attention, and brands are becoming harder than ever to ignore. Brands are more prevalent in our lives today than they were in the 1980s and 1990s, but as consumers, we still want to believe that we are not influenced by brands, or that, in any case, we are free to make choices between competing brands.

It's well known that competition makes a brand grow stronger. A brand that's number two (or number one with a chaser) has to prove itself constantly.

Customers critiquing big brands is nothing new. People have enjoyed wearing T-shirts with rude variations on famous logos since at least the 1960s. Organizations such as Adbusters have gone one step further, doctoring billboards to subvert the corporate brand message. Though such actions are criticized as juvenile and illegal, the fact is, they draw attention to the hypocrisy and cynicism of some brands' advertising, and are remembered by both customers and corporations long after they disappear. One would like to think that big-brand advertisers have learned their lesson: you can't say things that are hypocritical or cynically manipulative of your audience.

In 2000, anticapitalism reached a zenith with the publication of Naomi Klein's book *No Logo*. Her attack on the labor and marketing practices of the companies

Consumer backlash
Video screenshots from "iPod's Dirty Secret." The Neistat brothers decided to "take revenge" on Apple for refusing to replace a battery that failed after 18 months. Apple quickly changed its policy to protect the popularity of its brand.

Anticommercialism

Culturejammers.org have used the media tools of major brands to send a message of resistance. The "stars" in the flag consist of a rogue's gallery of the world's top 30 brands. But big brands, which continue trading as usual in the shop next to the billboard, easily ignore unfocused activities such as this.

Public opposition

Microsuck is the flagship site of the Microsoft Eradication Society, a public voicing of opposition to Microsoft's business practices.

Announcing our new identity.

After four years of being known primarily as [ahem]Microsoft.com, the flagship site of the Microsoft Eradication Society now sports a new, slightly more family friendly name: Microsuck. And if you've come here expect the *old* Microsuck website, we regret to inform you that it more. After laying dormant for a while, the previous owne offered it for sale to us. We couldn't resist.

Either way, we know that regular visitors to either site ma seeking some more details. And that's why we're so kindly offering to tell you more about the site's new name.

Microsuck@WWDC2003

behind some of the world's biggest brands caused a storm. The book was rebutted in the *Economist*, which pointed out that, rather than exploiting consumers, brands are required to earn their trust, and therefore are a tool by which consumers can hold corporations accountable. Contamination scandals involving Coca-Cola in places such as Belgium, Poland, and India forced the company to be honest with consumers and take steps to ensure product safety, because the company was concerned about the reputation of its brand.

Going to the other extreme, some marketers have complained about what they call the "tyranny of the consumer." Chris Anderson, founding editor of *Wired* magazine, told an audience, "Your brand is what Google says your brand is, not what you say your brand is," apparently meaning that any disgruntled consumer with a grudge can use the web to tear down years of accumulated goodwill.

It's true that in this age of radio talk shows, ubiquitous e-mail, and weblogs, accountability is being demanded more than ever. But corporations are realizing that they can use the same tools to defend themselves and recover their reputations.

And finally, buying behavior is still based on emotion, not a rational weighing of the information at hand. The anti-iPod video/website, ipodsdirtysecret.com, presented some damning information about a flaw in Apple's star product. Apple fixed the issue, and it doesn't seem to have had any measurable impact on iPod sales or brand perceptions. Sites like ihatestarbucks.com and www.microsuck.com have also had an impact.

Customers can influence brand meaning by positive actions as well as negative. Remixes, mash-ups, and spontaneous "crossover appeal," where a brand is adopted by an unexpected audience, are more and more a fact of life for brands. Savvy companies take advantage of this and set up their production for mass customization or actual co-creation of products, as has LEGO Factory, which gives customers the opportunity to design, share, and buy their own custom LEGO models.

Certainly, web technology has given customers greater power to respond to producers. We are entering an age in which successful, lasting brands will be those that harness customers' ideas and make them a permanent part of brand development.

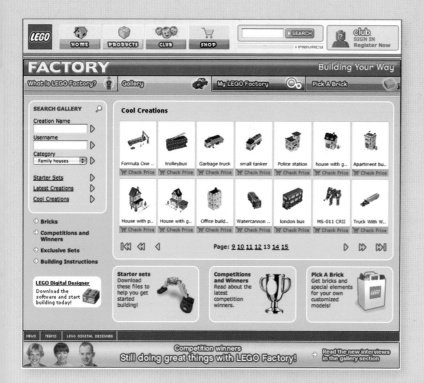

Involving the customer
Website screenshot of LEGO Factory tools. Mass customization and co-creation at work. LEGO now lets customers design their own models using freely downloadable tools. The pieces needed to build the model can be ordered as a kit from LEGO, which then adds the model to its catalog for sale to the public.

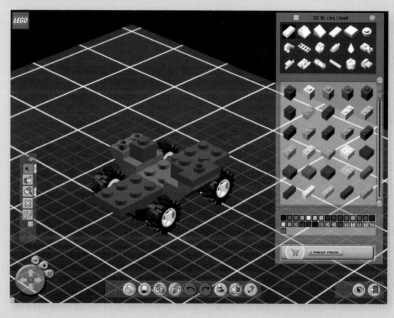

Brand consulting and the future of brands

"Factories rust away, packages become obsolete, products lose their relevance. But great brands live forever."

Backer Spielvogel Bates motto

The discipline of branding is the love child of graphic design, advertising, marketing, PR, and corporate identity. A branding consultancy competes with all of these businesses for both respect and clients—and often finds it must cooperate with all of those fields to do its job. Branding specialists also have to work alongside niche firms in fields like naming, web programming, prototype fabrication, sign making, direct mailing, call-center services, and event planning.

At the top of the market, competition comes from the giants of management consulting who can offer their multinational clients advice about branding along with other areas such as change management, process re-engineering, and IT.

What can a firm dedicated to branding offer a client that the others can't? Mostly, the ability to tie all the strings together and bring a multidisciplinary view to brand projects. As in the old fable of the short-sighted creatures who could only see parts of the elephant (its leg, its tusks, its trunk, an eye), brand consulting fulfills the vital role of seeing the whole beast.

In *The 22 Immutable Laws of Branding*, Al Ries writes that a brand like Kodak ought to be allowed to die because it lacks what he terms "credibility" outside the area of film, which has been made obsolete by digital photography. But this argument overlooks the essence of what has made Kodak a great brand. It transcends its product, film, to stand for something more universally appealing—capturing memories. That, of course, can be done on any medium. Kodak may yet fail to make the leap from film to digital, but effective brand consulting would help it succeed. A consultant would have to unite change management, manufacturing, and PR, along with areas such as alternative marketing, to ensure that the values which made Kodak a great brand for film can persist into the digital age.

And where is the discipline of branding headed? Undoubtedly, a brand manager will need to master alternative branding techniques, such as network marketing and brand integration in entertainment and games. As traditional advertising and PR decline in impact, these new techniques will be much in demand by brands desperate to gain a toehold in consumers' lives.

Traditional branding is still important in developing countries. The economies of countries such as India, Brazil, Russia, Indonesia, and China—to name a handful

Branding in Asia

In many Asian nations, such as India, local brands are successfully following the model of European and American consumer brands. Brands such as Ayush and Lakmé, from Hindustan Lever Ltd., also have the opportunity to draw on the rich and deep legacies of Asia's many beautiful cultures.

of the biggest—are just beginning to exploit the power of brands to add value to their manufacturing and services, and to benefit exports. Marcello Minale, the Chairman of Minale Tattersfield Design Strategy, observes that in developed countries like the UK, truly challenging opportunities in branding are becoming rare. So many brands are well established—and so many capable designers and branding experts are ready to serve them—that most jobs call for an incremental makeover at best. As can be seen from the Minale portfolio (see pages 204–13), the exciting projects that call for an end-to-end branding solution tend to be in places like the Middle East, Asia, and South America.

In a discussion of African brands on the Kenyan website www.brandscape.co.ke, Fanis Nyangayi, owner of Target Marketing in Tanzania, wrote, "We marketers have actually been spending time building other people's brands while having none of our own to be proud of." Local brands will grow, and this will undoubtedly change.

Brand managers in developing countries have one huge advantage over earlier generations of their counterparts in the West: they can draw readily on a wide body of know-how, much of it shared freely via the Internet. In online discussion forums such as brandchannel.com (run by Interbrand) and marketingprofs.com, many of the most avid readers and contributors are residents of countries in which the transition from commodity exports to value-added marketing and manufacturing is now underway. In the future, as these countries feel the pressure to differentiate what they make, and to build demand for their offerings in the face of new exports from poorer nations, brands will play a deciding role.

Westward expansion
Nanjing-MG in China produce kits of a revised version of the TF roadster for shipping to the UK, and Nanjing Automobile are looking into assembling local versions of Nanjing-MG sports cars for the Russian market.

Brands on the rise

Brands to watch in the twenty-first century include rising stars from Asia, Africa, and Latin America. These are becoming increasingly visible, and popular, around the globe. Lenovo computers, along with both Chery and Geely cars, all from China, are examples of brands whose best days are yet to come.

Anatomy

A logo is not a brand, a name is not a brand, nor is a product design, a package design, a visual identity, an advertising jingle, or a shopping experience. These things are all merely the tangible aspects of a complex sign system whose goal is to put an intangible—but powerful—brand idea or insight into the mind of a customer.

The notion of brand insight is far more fundamental than the readily recognizable elements of a brand identity such as the logo, the package design, or the advertising. The insight can refer to a personal goal, an emotional response, affinity with a set of values, or a dream of a better future. What's more, the insight doesn't need to relate to the product in question. The insight behind the Coca-Cola brand, for example, is inclusion in a worldwide family, which really has nothing to do with sugar water.

The magic of branding is to utilize all the devices of a brand identity to tie the product to the insight. Magic (as practiced on stage, at least) is all about perceptions, and so is branding.

First the brand is given a name, then a visual style, a tone of voice, rules of engagement, then all the other elements of a systematic identity. Each element has a specific part to play; the pieces can come together in different ways for different kinds of brands, in different sectors. If a brand is well crafted, then all its pieces reinforce one another and the association between idea and identity is a strong one. Experiencing any one element of the identity (the swirling script, the curvy bottle, the red can) will trigger recollection of the whole, along with the intended viewer response—a desire for the branded product or service.

Understanding the role of each element in a brand identity, and knowing how to craft it in just the right way to elicit just the right response, demands an understanding of the customer more than anything else. This comes from observation and experience. Whether you are an entrepreneur, manager, or designer, creating a successful brand means knowing how your customers perceive each element of your brand identity, and helping them connect those to grasp the brand insight.

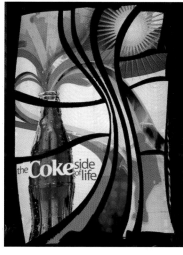
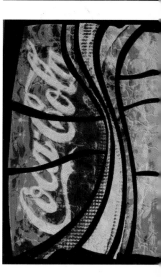

Core benefits and positioning

At the heart of every brand, the customer expects to find a product or service that matches what is promised. The first thing to grasp when setting out to build a new brand is, what is great about this thing?

In a great product, the benefit should be obvious. Sometimes, however, a little vision and imagination are required in order to articulate them properly. The story of one of the oldest brands, Ivory soap, is instructive.

In 1878, when James Gamble, of Procter & Gamble fame, developed an inexpensive soap to compete with high-quality, imported Castile soaps (made purely from vegetable oils), he announced that it was "satisfactory in every respect," and would be called P&G White Soap. His partner, Harley Procter, insisted they think of a more distinctive brand name. He found his inspiration in Psalm 45:8, "All thy garments smell of myrrh and aloes and cassia, out of the ivory palaces whereby they have made thee glad."

To prove the quality of Ivory soap, Procter & Gamble sent samples out to chemists for scientific testing. The results were tabulated, and one tester reported finding a total of only 0.56% non-soap impurities in his sample. The company seized on this and for years marketed Ivory soap as "99 and 44/100 percent pure."

In the early years, another benefit used to promote Ivory soap was the fact that it floats. The buoyancy doesn't get you any cleaner, but it does prevent you losing the soap in murky water. This happy accident occurred when an early batch was overwhipped. Customers ordered more of the "floating soap." P&G realized they had another benefit to differentiate Ivory from its competitors, and it became a regular feature. To this day, P&G remains open to customer feedback to help the company understand its products' benefits as customers perceive them.

As the twentieth century progressed, the marketing of Ivory became more sophisticated. Ads featuring the "Ivory lady" set a standard for female glamour; no longer was the benefit in the soap, but in a carefully idealized image of the user. This process of moving up to a higher level of brand benefits is known as laddering, and is key to many brands' success. Once customers are familiar

with its basic benefits, the brand moves up the ladder to a more lifestyle-centered, more intuitive and emotional appeal. This also makes it harder for new competitors to get started.

Many products aim only to be "affordable," or "economy." Brands at the lower end of the market use design and packaging to say to the customer, "I'm not the best, but I don't cost much." There are enough customers who avoid expensive-looking brands that such products do very well. Other brands go for the very top of the market, positioned where better-off customers will find them. They promise, without apology, "You're going to pay more, but you'll know it was worthwhile." Many such brands are deliberately understated, and lower- and middle-income consumers often aren't even aware of them.

Most brands try to appeal to the middle, appearing fancy yet remaining within reach. They use a judicious mix of design, pricing, packaging, and merchandising to offer a clear message about benefits, values, affirmation, and satisfaction of desire.

Market positioning

Although Kiehl's packaging is so understated it looks generic, the styling of the backgrounds in these images makes it clear that the intended customer is decidedly well off (after all, Kiehl's sells horse-care products too!) Other factors, such as pricing and sales exclusively in Kiehl's boutiques or on the web, reinforce the upmarket positioning.

Added benefits

Procter & Gamble started their Ivory soap brand in the 1870s. At first, the advertised benefits related to the purity and buoyancy of the product; later, to the glamorous image of the idealized user.

Insight

"When you are armed with a powerful insight, the ideas never stop flowing," writes Phil Dusenberry, former chairman of BBDO North America, in his 2005 memoir *Then We Set His Hair on Fire* (the book title refers to the infamous accident during the filming of Michael Jackson's commercial for Pepsi).

Dusenberry draws an important distinction between insight and idea: an insight is a grasp of the fundamental truth that sets one brand apart from its competitors, where ideas illustrate the insight so that everyone else can grasp it too.

Dusenberry gives the example of his brand claim for General Electric. "We bring good things to life." This slogan went beyond the obvious fact that GE was so pervasive, making everything from lightbulbs to toasters to railroad engines to nuclear reactors. The key insight was not that GE makes everything, but rather, that the things GE makes make life better. Simple as it sounds, Dusenberry's rivals in the ad business had failed to get it. Hundreds of good ideas flowed from this insight, which endured as a slogan for nearly a quarter of a century.

George Lois, the iconoclastic creative adman, laid out much the same manifesto a decade and a half earlier, in his 1991 book *What's the Big Idea?* He cites the legendary campaign by Doyle Dane Bernbach for the original Volkswagen, the "people's car" that Hitler had developed in the 1930s. The ads—headlined Think Small, Beetle, and Lemon—are still famous nearly half a century later.

Lois recalls a conversation he had in his New York office when coming up with the big idea for Volkswagen (VW). "I figured out the marketing problem. We have to sell a Nazi car in a Jewish town." Lois and his partner Julian König solved the problem by making all the perceived negatives of VW—its size, funny shape, etc—appealing through the use of charming, irreverent humor. The Beetle became an icon.

Many companies have re-examined themselves to gain the vital insight that makes their brands stand out. Kone makes escalators, elevators, and automatic doors. When the firm wanted to strengthen its brand, it began by repositioning itself as an "accessibility" company. That makes perfect sense: all of its products allow you to get from one place to another inside a building.

Why the need to redefine Kone's benefits and position? The new way of looking at the company provided a heightened insight into its benefits from the user's point of view. As an escalator-and-elevator company, Kone was indistinguishable from its competitors. With the insight of providing accessibility, it raised its position to category leader, with the added emotional appeal gained from the suggestion that its products assist the disadvantaged.

In the 1990s, when rebranding was a fashionable management buzzword, some companies tried to reposition themselves in ways that were more silly than insightful. The insight at the heart of a brand must be simple, focused, and truthful, as simple as "this is the best." Then the ideas that flow from it begin to build an emotional bond with the customer.

Think small.

Our little car isn't so much of a novelty any more. A couple of dozen college kids don't try to squeeze inside it. The guy at the gas station doesn't ask where the gas goes. Nobody even stares at our shape. In fact, some people who drive our little flivver don't even think 32 miles to the gallon is going any great guns. Or using five pints of oil instead of five quarts. Or never needing anti-freeze. Or racking up 40,000 miles on a set of tires. That's because once you get used to some of our economies, you don't even think about them any more. Except when you squeeze into a small parking spot. Or renew your small insurance. Or pay a small repair bill. Or trade in your old VW for a new one. Think it over.

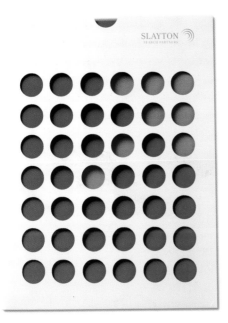

Unique customer appeal
Insight allows a company to establish a unique position for its brand, and appeal to customers in a way that transcends the limitations of its product category. Volkswagon's brand is more than a small car—it is about looking at life in a lovingly irreverent manner.

Market differentiation
Brand identity by Infinia. In the business of executive research, comparatively little attention has been paid to brand differentiation among firms. Infinia determined that Slayton could occupy a significant niche position. They offered all the reassuring resources and experience of a large firm, together with the specialized knowledge and nimbleness of a smaller, boutique operation, all united by their responsiveness and quick thinking. By articulating this insight and presenting it through a well-developed identity, Slayton was able to capture a unique niche in the market.

Ideas

An idea can take form in various ways. It is the unique design that makes a product useful and fun. It is the clever packaging concept that promises something the competition doesn't. It is the unforgettable advertising claim (also known as a tagline, strapline, slogan, or sign-off). It is the visual motif that drives the campaign. It is the web interface that gives customers exactly what they want. It is the pleasant surprise from the customer-service representative.

Ideas should not be confused with insight: insight is perennial, while good ideas can and should change regularly. An idea is the innovation that keeps a product relevant to a customer's life and keeps the customer involved with the brand. Ideas usually have a life cycle of a few years at most. Ideas are the visible manifestations of the brand, and assuming the insight is well founded, good ideas should flow almost effortlessly.

The difference between brand insight and ideas can be seen in the following examples:

• The ad agency BBDO was able to build a quarter-century's worth of GE campaigns upon its insight about users' lives being improved by myriad GE products. The insight was summed up with the claim, "We bring good things to life." Ideas for individual commercials and advertisements flowed out of this insight by the dozen. Nearly 25 years later, the basic insight was still valid, but a fresh, twenty-first-century expression was called for. "Imagination at work" was judged to fit the bill.

• An iPod is simply a small, external hard drive. The idea of turning it into a latter-day Walkman rests on the insight that Apple makes technology easy, integrating hassle-free downloading, browsing, and listening.

• New ideas for Ben & Jerry's ice cream flavors are submitted by fans on the company website. One recent winner: Puttin' On a Ritz, consisted of vanilla ice cream, caramel, and Ritz crackers. The insight behind the brand is that everyone can get involved in social responsibility (and enjoy good ice cream).

• Charles Schwab's investment products and services stem from the insight that the Internet can be used to give individual investors straightforward, personalized service while reducing commissions and fees. The brand identity emphasizes the personal relationship, which is attractive to institutional investment clients as well.

The rapid pace of pop culture encourages us to expect new ideas all the time. Insight alone won't sustain a brand forever: we quickly tire of brands that have "run out of ideas." Brands need both the solid foundation of a great insight and the steady flow of new ideas to remain compelling.

Quality and tradition

Design by Irving. The idea behind the packaging for this range of children's biscuits stems from the insight that it is the traditional methods and quality ingredients that Artisan Biscuits uses that set the brand apart. The visual style conveys a sense of handcrafting, while the illustrations selected, a different one for each flavor, are based on traditional children's stories. Each box contains a copy of the story illustrated on its cover.

Values

It's not hard for a brand to be aligned with certain values. Being aligned with the right ones can give a boost to customer loyalty. Values are the things a brand stands for. Customers are generally savvy enough to perceive a brand's values through the behavior of its corporate parent; actions speak louder than PR. Values should be fundamental to a brand's self: they are precisely what keep a brand from being superficial or trivial. Nonetheless, it is not always apparent to customers just what values a brand stands for.

Integrity is commonly espoused, but not always adhered to. Companies can spend years building up an image of integrity, only to see it torn down by a single act of foolishness—for example, knowingly shipping customers a shoddy product, mistreating workers, hiding financial malfeasance, or polluting the environment. Hypocrisy makes any PR disaster all the more damaging; brand stewards, from the CEO down, must take care always to act on their values, rather than just talking about them.

A **commitment to excellence** is something else companies talk about, though fewer seem to know how to make excellence a cornerstone of their brand. Tom Peters, the management expert, defined excellence as (among other things) a never-ending quest for improvement in processes and results, being close to customers, allowing employees to use their own smarts, and developing a culture of innovation. All of the companies that Peters discussed in his book *In Search of Excellence* had exceptional achievements, but for various reasons, not all have survived. Excellence is not a simple formula; it also takes luck, and perhaps more of a focus on brand dialogue than Peters and his coauthor, Robert Waterman, realized at that time.

Customer responsiveness means never having your customers feel that you don't care about them. How are customer complaints handled in your company? Are problems solved quickly and satisfactorily? Unfortunately, many big firms see customer service as a cost—a necessary evil—rather than an opportunity to build lasting, lucrative relationships with thousands of loyal customers. The lack of a corporate culture of responsiveness leads to a higher rate of "churn," in which customers come and go, which is costly. A company like Amazon. com, which is built on the compulsion of its founder, Jeff Bezos, to provide the best customer care, can boast of customers who have been loyal to it for over 10 years. In Internet time, this is literally forever.

The founders of Ben & Jerry's ice cream felt strongly that social responsibility and the good treatment of workers was important. So important that, for the first several years, the highest-paid employees (Ben Cohen and Jerry Greenfield themselves) limited their pay to five times that of the lowest-paid employee. The company, despite now being owned by multinational giant Unilever, still adheres to values such as social responsibility and support of environmental causes through its use of natural ingredients. In 2006, Ben & Jerry's was criticized for using eggs from caged hens. This was never an issue with other ice-cream makers, but because of the values espoused by Ben & Jerry's, customers felt such practices were at odds with the brand. Ben & Jerry's responded later that year by announcing a "total transition" to egg suppliers who raise cage-free hens using humane methods—an excellent example of brand dialogue.

Brand conscience
Part of the appeal of Ben & Jerry's ice cream is its strong association with liberal social values: combating the effects of global warming, supporting fair trade in buying coffee and other raw materials, and only using eggs from Certified Humane Raised & Handled, cage-free hens.

Offset the global warming impact of your air travel by supporting renewable energy projects. Click here to learn more.

Fair Trade Certified™ products directly support a better life for farming families in the developing world through fair prices, community development projects, and eco-friendly farming practices. For the full scoop, please click here!

We're making a transition to egg suppliers who use "Certified-Humane," cage-free methods to raise their egg-laying hens. We're excited to be the first national food manufacturer to move towards this goal. Click here to learn more.

Lifestyle

Advertising agencies have known for years that one of the best ways to sell a brand is to position it as a vital part of a lifestyle that customers aspire to. Every society can be broken down into segments, or so the theory goes, and the defining characteristics of each segment can be used to build an attractive picture of how customers could live if they bought the products being sold.

More recent thinking, however, suggests that segments are not always so clear-cut, and that there are so many segments that producers cannot possibly tailor a product to fit them all. In any case, customers nowadays feel free to reassign products to lifestyle categories not intended by their marketers. In the US, for example, New Era baseball caps became a hit with urban youths who were not baseball fans.

Cultural elements of an urban, youthful lifestyle were exploited by Sprite when the soft-drink brand began aggressively sponsoring urban music, with a focus on remixes by popular hip-hop DJs. The idea of remixing fitted in well with the new flavors Sprite was introducing. Numerous musical events and CD releases were emblazoned with the Sprite name and logo. The aim was to fix the Sprite brand in customers' minds as the refreshment for anyone who aspires to an image of hip-hop chic.

An active lifestyle centered around individual sports and exercise is attractive not only to those who buy sporting gear and clothes, but also to those who dream of greater personal achievement. Lance Armstrong, seven-times Tour de France winner and cancer survivor, has applied his personal brand to a number of initiatives—from charities to investments—whose appeal lies as much in their invocation to lead an active, optimistic life as in Armstrong's personal popularity.

Many advertisements for pharmaceuticals, real estate, and financial services paint a rosy picture of the retiree lifestyle, in which fit and smiling 60-somethings enjoy life to the fullest, usually outdoors. The implication is that the product being sold will contribute to this mythic sense of comfort and wellness at any age—the appeal to the over-50s may be persuasive, but it is so pervasive that one must wonder if its purpose is to differentiate or to reassure, without concern for the brand.

One of the things that make "cult" brands so successful is that they seem to define a lifestyle all their own: Apple defines the digital lifestyle, Harley-Davidson the "easy rider" lifestyle, Starbucks the "latte liberal" lifestyle, etc.

Bringing the brand to life
Brands can try to ingratiate themselves with potential customers in a number of ways. One is by portraying a chosen lifestyle in their advertising; another is to sponsor music, sporting events, or other activities that will get the brand seen and experienced in a positive light by the target group. Sprite introduced new flavors intended to appeal to urban (especially black) consumers, and sponsored the release of hip-hop music sampler CDs, heavily branded with the visual identity of the new flavors. It also sponsored live music events with some of the artists involved.

Magazine brands were once powerful definers of readers' lifestyles. *Esquire* and *Playboy* defined the lifestyle of the young man with aspirations and disposable income from the 1930s to the 1970s. *Cosmopolitan* and *Ms.* defined the lifestyles of young women seeking to liberate themselves from old stereotypes from the 1960s to the 1980s

However, the power of mainstream magazines has declined as the media/industrial complex gives way to the new networked economy of the twenty-first century. In the 2000s, it is more often niche titles that seize the opportunity to present, in both editorial and advertising content, a specific lifestyle built around brands.

Brand personality

Every brand can be anthropomorphized to a certain degree. That doesn't mean every brand needs a little mascot character with big eyes and a funny name; it means that at the heart of every brand is a set of characteristics, akin to a human personality, that customers can relate to as if the brand were a real companion. Words like "honest," "inspiring," "sympathetic," "reassuring," "fun," "intelligent," and "supportive" often crop up when passionate customers describe their favorite brands. We tend to see human attributes, that is, personality, in things we want to have a relationship with.

How a brand is projected, visually as well as through a specific voice, needs to be consistent across all areas in order for customers to see its personality. One of the common mistakes many brands make is to project a well-crafted personality in their advertising, but quite a different personality, or none whatsoever, in "below the line" areas such as customer billing materials.

While the heart of any brand has to be a worthwhile, quality product, there's no question that having an endearing personality can make up for a few flaws. Friends—and customers—are willing to overlook shortcomings if the personality is attractive. A great brand offers a producer the luxury of a second chance.

The quickest way to attach a personality to a brand is through a celebrity endorsement. The pop star Britney Spears has attached her name to two perfumes, Curious and Fantasy, creating instant appeal for products that would otherwise have had a hard time gaining attention in a crowded market. The risk is that, as Spears has run into difficulties in her personal life, so the products could end up being tarnished. A brand that desires longevity would do better to build its own personality, rather than adopting a celebrity's.

Creating brand character
Snapple started out as three friends bottling apple juice in a garage in New York City. With hand-drawn labels that imparted an irreverent sense of humor, the brand grew popular. Now owned by a large corporation, Snapple maintains its personality through humorous little details, trivia facts printed under the cap, and promotions that emphasize a sense of fun. In a similar vein, Google offers users an occasional surprise in the form of thematic doodles or drawings that replace part or all of the logo on special days. Of course, brand personalities can be suave or serious as well.

Perhaps the best personality trait for a brand is self-confidence. A good salesman says, "What kind of car do you want to buy today?" moving quickly past the issue of whether you even want to buy anything at all. Likewise, a confident brand doesn't merely offer itself; like an innocent puppy it assumes you want it, and sells you on its personality. Confidence is displayed in many ways: cheerful humor, cool detachment, a free sample, or an emphasis on image while downplaying information.

Snapple, a maker of fruit and tea drinks, uses bright colors and whimsy on its labels, including occasionally turning the logo upside down, to convey a cheerful confidence.

"Cool" is a trait that many brands aspire to, though few really pull it off. Often, it is the associations more than the product itself that make a brand cool. Luxury goods trade on coolness and their association with a high-class lifestyle.

Google is a supremely self-assured brand. The company is one of the most profitable in the world, even though millions of users have never paid a penny for its services. Its super-simple, uncluttered design, occasionally enlivened with a carefree doodle in honor of a special day, reflects this bold confidence.

Product design

Product design concerns both functionality and aesthetics. With a few notable exceptions, it often seems as though manufacturers have neglected one in favor of the other; few products score well on both. The idea of combining great design and great function seems to have begun with modernist designers of furniture and cars, eventually spreading to consumer electronics, athletic equipment, and consumer products in general.

Firms that do manage to get both the aesthetics and the function right become synonymous with great brands: Apple, Bang & Olufsen, Braun, Herman Miller, IKEA, Nike, Nokia, Philips, and Sony. The secret is to start thinking about the branding and design early in the development process. What values and benefits should the customer expect? What cultural standards will the customer use to judge the product? If answers to these questions are agreed upon early, the design process will yield much more satisfactory results.

Samsung is a textbook example of this approach. In the late 1980s, this Korean company was manufacturing undistinguished, commodity electronics. Worldwide sales were decent, but price pressure was so intense that profit margins were slim. Samsung decided the answer lay in solving the mystery of design, and set out to find what would appeal to global consumers.

The company's first step was to send designers and engineers around the world to learn about what appeals to different cultures' tastes, and to try and grasp exactly what distinguishes original and innovative design from the generic look that is typical of commodity electronics. This exploratory

Product options
With the release of the BeoLab 4 loudspeaker, Bang & Olufsen continued its tradition of combining attractive design with great sound quality. The BeoLab 4 is available with a range of stand options for the wall, floor, or table ceiling, and its cloth covers are available in four colors.

learning period lasted many months. Largely as a result of these efforts, trying to see design through the cultural background of their prospective customers, Samsung's high-tech electronics business was able to grow and innovate at a rapid rate in the 1990s and 2000s. Interbrand named Samsung the fastest-growing global brand, with a valuation rising 96.25% from 2001 to 2004.

Nokia, ranked by Interbrand as one of the top 10 brands worldwide for several years in a row, has also built its brand largely on the strength of its product design. Motorola, which lagged behind other cell-phone makers in the early 2000s, was able to revive its fortunes by overhauling its product design. In the meantime, other cell-phone makers that had been market leaders dropped off the chart, or, like Sony and Ericsson, were forced to join together in order to survive.

Top: Product as fashion
Nokia has become famous for introducing new cell-phone handsets at the rate of what seems like one every five minutes. Some of the latest models barely resemble telephones, but their designs identify them all very clearly as Nokia. The 7373, designed by Giambattista Valli, takes the idea of the phone as fashion accessory to new heights.

Above and left: Form and function
The successful blending of form and function has perhaps reached its zenith in cell-phone design; brands like Nokia, Motorola, and Samsung have succeeded by making highly functional phones that double as fashion accessories.

Name

Before anything else—logo, packaging, or advertising—a brand needs a name. The name is the thing by which a brand is remembered and discussed. A "good name" is synonymous with a good reputation. It is comparatively easy for a brand to change its logo, its package design, or its advertising; it is much harder to change a name and get customers to connect the new name with the old one. Brands that pick a good name find half the marketing and branding work is done for them. "The best product and company names require the least advertising. They are advertisements," reads the website of San Francisco–based naming agency Igor.

Sounds are not neutral; they have intrinsic associations, and it is important that a brand name have the right sounds to conjure the right associations. Making matters tricky is the fact that those associations shift from one culture to another. A name that may sound good to French ears can sound peculiar to Germans, and vice versa. A short, likable name that can be easily pronounced in many languages (and registered as an Internet domain in every country) has a huge advantage today.

Igor defines four types of name, paraphrased here with their permission:

- **functional** or descriptive names that literally describe what the company, product, or service offers, e.g., General Motors, British Petroleum, American Telephone & Telegraph;
- **invented** names, either with Latin/Greek roots, or based on fun, rhythmic sounds, e.g., Jeep, Viagra, Google, Exxon;
- **experiential** names, similar to descriptive names, but focused on the experience rather than the function, e.g., Hungry Man (frozen dinners), Land Rover (all-terrain four-wheel drives), Fidelity (investments); and
- **evocative** names, selected to evoke confidence or strength, e.g., Jaguar, Mach3, and Lucent (telecommunications).

There are also **referential** names, which refer directly to a founder or place of origin. Examples include Ford, Harley-Davidson, Hewlett-Packard, Guinness, and Evian. Another category is **acronyms**, for example IBM, USX, BP, and EMI. Most of these initials once stood for something, but for the consumer, their significance has been lost.

The power of a name
A perfect brand name, Silk
at once denotes the product,
soy milk, and connotes
favorable associations
with smoothness and luxury.
It seems unlikely that any
competitor in its category
could come up with anything
better, giving Silk an advantage
stronger than any advertising.

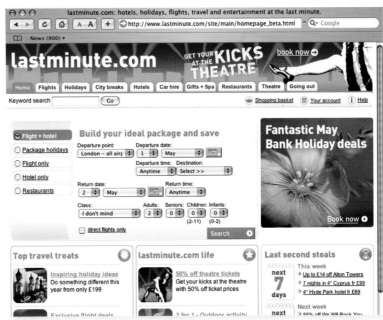

Functional names
lastminute.com is a great
functional name: it is simple
and memorable, and suggests
at once both Internet service
and spur-of-the-moment
decisions and bookings.

Evocative names
The idea behind Innocent drinks was to make it easy for people to do themselves some good: Innocent's founders wanted people to think of the drinks as their one healthy habit. The name Innocent picks up on this, and also conveys the fact that the drinks are pure and unadulterated.

The best names—the most memorable ones—tend to be both invented and evocative; in rare cases, functional and experiential too. Such names dominate their product or service category: it becomes virtually impossible for a competitor to think of a better name. In *The Brand Gap*, Marty Neumeier lists seven criteria for a good name: brevity, distinctiveness, appropriateness, easy spelling and pronunciation, likability, extendability, and protectability.

Most firms struggle to get their names into the public consciousness and achieve the wide recognition they desire. For a bemused few, however, the problem is the opposite: their name is so handy and perfect for the product or service, it is adopted by the public and becomes a generic term. When this happens, the owner of the brand name is in danger of losing the rights to it as a trademark, since generic names of things cannot be trademarked. The list of former trademarks that are now common words is a long one (corn flakes, linoleum, aspirin …) and the list of currently endangered names is just as long: Kleenex, Xerox, FedEx, Google …

Brand names encounter the biggest problems when they cross borders. Federal Express found it expedient to shorten their name: research showed that "federal" had negative connotations in some countries, while some Asians had difficulty with the *r* and *l*. There are many humorous tales of marketers who fail to research all the evocations a name can have in a local language, and end up with a failure.

Some brands choose a completely different name when they cross borders. The Snickers bar was renamed Marathon when it was first sold in the UK because marketers thought the American name sounded like "knickers." Eventually, the American name was adopted, and Marathon was reused as the name of another, high-energy bar from the same company.

Most products have several names: the manufacturer's name, the line, the product, a plain-language identifier, and perhaps a subidentifier such as size, flavor, or color. This can be confusing.

Progress and competitiveness push some companies to update product names regularly. Gillette introduced the three-blade Mach3 razor in 1997. A few years later an improved version arrived, called the Mach3 Turbo. Now Gillette also offers the battery-powered M3Power and M3Power Nitro. What began as a simple name, with manly evocations of speed, has accumulated generic add-ons that are crushing the original name and risk undermining any loyalty that customers might have built up toward the original Mach3.

Apple was falling into the same trap in the 1990s, with names as unwieldy as the Power Macintosh Performa 6400, but smartly retreated. All models now have a short, friendly name such as iBook or Mac Mini, depending on the basic category, with no clunky add-ons to designate processor speed or bus type. These designations may be important to some customers, but they shouldn't clutter up the name. If it isn't memorable, it isn't a good name.

Logo

We've seen that a brand is what ties an insight and its name together, but although we think and communicate verbally, we orient ourselves in our surroundings primarily by visual means. So beyond the name, a brand identity requires a visual system, beginning with a logo.

"Logo" comes from the Greek *logos*, meaning "word." It is a shortened form of the slightly old-fashioned "logotype," which means "word form." The logo is the name given form—that is, made visual. It is the distinctive mark that works in the context of its environment to evoke the brand insight in the viewer's mind, playing off the viewer's own experience and also reinforcing that experience in preparation for the next encounter. However, a logo is not a brand—it is shorthand for one. First comes the brand insight; then the logo. Too many start-up companies get this backward.

Nowadays few logos are truly original in appearance. What is more important is that they evoke the desired associations and emotional response in the viewer. A historical or cultural allusion can be desirable in a logo, especially if it is a new logo for an old brand, or a new brand resulting from a merger or acquisition that wishes to retain some of the equity from the brand(s) it replaces. If a brand is to appear fresh and compelling, it needs to contain visual cues that reflect the styles and techniques of the moment. What it gives up in originality, a logo can gain in relevance—at least, for a time.

Form-wise, what makes a good logo? The designer Paul Rand wrote, "The ideal logo is simple, elegant, economical, flexible, practical, and unforgettable." The selection of an appropriate form is a subjective process. It is virtually impossible today to fulfill Rand's criteria with a unique, novel form, and many new logos are bound to remind viewers of others they have seen. Still, a logo should aim to be distinct from others in its category, to avoid clichés, and above all to avoid infringing someone else's trademark.

A logo can take almost any form. Some logos are simply a word. Others are a wordless symbol. Most involve some combination of the two. Many logos have multiple variants of shape or color. The important thing is that customers recognize them and receive the desired impression.

The best logos, like national flags, exert an emotional pull on the viewer. Certain symbols may also carry deeper meanings that can be appropriated for a brand. For example, the psychologist Carl Jung saw the star as a symbol of the spiritual part of the psyche, that part of the personality which survives death. Hence, a logo that incorporates a star can be a subconscious reminder of our aspirations to immortality.

By itself, a logo is just a mark, but it acquires meaning through a lifetime of stories and experiences. A logo can change over time, but it should always keep its connection to the insights and meanings in customers' minds.

Below left: Visual cues
Simple pictograms, once they become familiar enough through repetition, can be read as names, like the universally recognized Apple apple and Nike swoosh. Whether a logo is a simple word, like Panasonic, a subtly rendered 3-D symbol, like the at&t globe, or bright and dynamic like this logo for the Port of Long Beach, it serves as a visual reminder of the brand insight, values, and benefits. This can take a variety of forms, depending on context. The precise form is not important, so long as the viewer can make the right association with the brand.

Below: Logo recognition
Even without being able to read the name, we recognize the brand represented by the symbol of the Golden Arches. It has been made familiar to us through advertising and signage around the world. The logo is associated in our minds not only with the name McDonald's, but also with the insights and experiences of the brand: the food, restaurants, and convenience, reinforced by its past and present taglines in various languages.

Color

In branding, there are several issues to consider concerning color. First, you need to master the physical aspects of color, which mostly have to do with graphic design: boldness, dynamic tension, legibility, and so on. Second, you need to consider how colors (and their combinations) make people feel. Certain colors have a soothing effect, while others have the opposite. Third, you must understand the cultural associations of certain colors. Is this color considered good luck in this country? Additionally, colors go in and out of fashion on a regular basis within any given market. Finally, it's important to master the science of color; to make sure the inks in the brochure match the plastics in the furniture, the graphics on the web, and the neon on the roof.

All of these issues will help answer a simple question: what difference will it make if a logo is red or green? You should be able to answer the corollaries, too: what impressions of the brand are evoked by the colors we choose for the packaging?

Why should we avoid using yellow in the advertising? Is it possible to have too many colors on the website?

Physics
Renaissance artists honed their color use meticulously, and handed down rules for using colors, based on physical laws, that we still respect. "Warm" colors (like red, yellow, and orange) appear to come forward in space, while "cool" colors (like blue, green, and purple) appear to recede. The judicious use of such colors in painting can give an impression of real depth.

Color combinations play other important roles as well. Contrasting tones increase the dynamic tension of an image. Color makes a page either inviting or aloof. The right (or wrong) combination can make a huge difference to the legibility of signs, billboards, websites, and brochures. Even a subtly discouraging color combination can put customers off a brand, while the right color scheme can prove irresistibly inviting.

Psychology

The psychological aspects of color have been mused upon since ancient times. Many artists and poets have bequeathed us their well-considered opinions. While a brand designer may consider these, a client's personal color likes and dislikes could well take precedence.

Tests have shown that people react to colors in predictable ways. Psychologists generally believe that our fundamental understanding of color is universal—white equates with purity, purple equates with passion—but opinions vary regarding how much our reactions are affected by culture.

Brands that can build up and exploit strong color associations can gain a valuable advantage because color can be a powerful brand mnemonic. Al and Laura Ries, in their book *The 22 Immutable Laws of Branding*, discuss the need for a brand to "own" its colors, not literally, but in the minds of customers. The Rieses cite McDonald's ownership of the red and yellow color combination, which leaves rival Burger King in a "me too" role with its red, yellow, and blue scheme. Color comes to be associated with a given brand in the customer's mind through long acclimatization. Brands should settle early in their lives on a simple scheme of one or two main colors that are unique in that category, and use them consistently.

Color recognition
When a brand makes optimal, consistent use of color, it can be said to "own" that color (or combination of colors), at least within its category. This can lead to recognition of the brand by color alone, even without the name and logo, and reinforcement of the brand identity on interiors, packaging, and livery by more subtle means. KLM has managed to "own" the color of the sky among airlines, so even if we cover up the logo, the aircraft is still recognizable. Yellow and black are dominant in the identity created for the Sprint mobile network by Lippincott Mercer.

Culture

Color interpretations depend strongly on culture. While it is traditional for brides to wear white in Western cultures, in Asia it is worn at funerals. To some eyes, white conveys elegance, to others it looks cheap; little green men are good luck in Ireland, bad luck in China.

It is important for any brand "going global" to be aware of such issues, and to adapt as necessary. The color component of any brand needs to be reconsidered in each local culture to be sure that it evokes the desired response. For example, when Minale Tattersfield was designing gas-station forecourts for a client in India, they proposed using green to denote environmental sensitivity. The client disagreed, feeling customers would be more likely to associate green with India's neighbor and national rival, Pakistan.

Science

Even after an appropriate color scheme is selected, the job is not done. Whole industries are devoted to the science of getting color right. A basic understanding of the technicalities of color perception is vital to dealing with some of the pitfalls of an effective branding program.

There's a physical difference between colors of light, such as those on a TV or computer screen, and reflected colors, like those on a printed page. These two "color spaces" are not the same, meaning that not every color that exists in one space can be faithfully reproduced in the other. In addition, colors that can be printed on paper using standard four-color process inks often can't be matched exactly with plastics or films, and vice versa: printed inks cannot match the rich, saturated hues of plastic or glass. The type of light available in different environments will also have an impact on how colors are seen. The life of a brand manager often consists of settling for approximations and compromises.

In the end, the important thing is the overall experience. Keep in mind that, while people have a good memory for colors and can often recall surprisingly subtle differences in shade, color is just one of the factors that make up a whole brand identity. So long as the other elements (type, photography, tone of voice, etc.) are consistent with expectations, customers will tolerate some deviation from a brand's "standard" shade.

Utilizing color symbolism
Red evokes excitement, stimulation, power, and aggression. It is the color of life, blood, and fire. Carl Jung wrote that it represents our desire to achieve an integrated personality; the psychologist Joan Kellogg found that patients who used red in art therapy were expressing a healthy desire for success.

Typeface

Type is the clothing that dresses words, giving them character, emphasis, and a subtle, but distinct personality that the reader often senses subconsciously.

Typography is the art of selecting and using an appropriate style of type, or font, in a way that reinforces the message of the words, without distracting from them. Text requires a typeface that is clear and legible—fancy letter shapes or ornaments distract the reader—but a big ad or store sign needs an eye-catching lettering style in order to stand out from the visual clutter and make a statement. Graphic designers are always coming up with new styles to meet both purposes.

Few people, even professional designers, can identify a font by name. Most people can, however, sense whether it looks exciting, reserved, modern, old-fashioned, edgy, tasteful, clear, or illegible; even design-illiterate customers get a sense of the values type reflects, if only subliminally.

Advertising agency creative teams tend to push to use the latest, hippest typefaces, often ignoring the standards outlined in clients' brand manuals. This can lead to the typographic design of the latest ad campaign looking quite different from, for example, the company's website.

While some degree of separation is unavoidable, the design of web pages and other materials (known in advertising parlance as "below the line") should be planned and executed so that customers perceive a connection with the advertising. Typographic consistency reinforces a brand identity; chaos hurts it.

Typographic consistency is necessary for long-lasting items, such as products and signage, that a customer may look at for years. Such items need to be timeless, without being generic, and consistent with established brand standards.

However, the type styles on short-term brand materials, such as ad campaigns and packaging, should show some sensitivity to current typographic fashions. The challenge for designers is to tread the difficult path between consistency and change so that, on the one hand, the brand image reflected in the typography stays recognizable, and on the other, it doesn't look out-of-date.

Some corporations spend thousands on the development of an original typeface for the exclusive use of that company's brand communications. In so doing, they are guaranteed that no one else's materials will have quite the same character as theirs, but they also lock themselves into using one font for a long time—perhaps too long.

Type personality
Phil Reynolds designed
by William Hall Design; ICFJ
designed by Siegel+Gale.
The choice of a particular
typeface is probably not
as important as the overall
quality of the typographic
treatment and the general
impression it conveys.

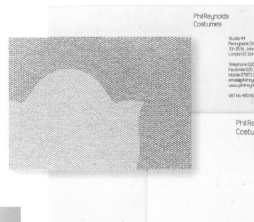

Visual style

Besides color and typography (see pages 92–7), visual style includes elements such as photography, illustration, and other graphic motifs, including borders and frames. Selecting the right kinds of visual elements can have a surprising impact on customer response to an advertisement or package design. As early as the 1930s, some marketers had an established wisdom about what customers liked to see in a brand; others, such as Louis Cheskin in Chicago, paid greater attention to researching how customers reacted to individual elements such as colors, shapes, materials, and the overall aesthetics of a given design.

Cheskin discovered, for example, that simple changes, such as packaging margarine in yellow instead of white, adding the outline of a spoon to a box of cake mix, or emphasizing modernist style in design after the launch of Sputnik in 1957, could all have a dramatic impact on sales. Cheskin was astute enough to realize that, while what he called "sensation transference" functioned in the short-term, over the long-term tastes change, and brands need to monitor their customers' responses constantly, and adapt accordingly.

Photography

Humans have communicated with pictures for far longer than they have with written words. It follows that realistic images are the most powerful element used in brand communication—stronger, perhaps, than the name, logo, colors, and type combined. In fact, when we speak of building a brand identity we speak of "image building."

Photographs or lifelike illustrations are the central focus of almost every advertisement and a good deal of packaging, especially where the contents are not visible. Very little brand communication consists of text only. The exceptions prove the rule—the very absence of images is sometimes used to send a message, because the lack of pictures is so striking.

Aside from the image elements that are apparent at first glance—content, composition, and style—images frequently use tricks to influence our perception, and contain cultural references, with varying degrees of subtlety, that reinforce (or inadvertently contradict) the intended meaning of the brand.

Some of the methods used to manipulate perception include angle, point of view, juxtaposition, lighting, focus, and coloration. Carmakers, for example, give their advertising agencies specific instructions on what angles their cars must be shot from in order to create the right impression of size and personality. Some soft-drink ads manipulate our deeply rooted psychological needs and fears (and thirst) by deliberate adjustment of our perspective in relation to the people in the ad. Light can focus attention and affect our feelings about a subject. Absolut vodka ads of the 1980s used this trick explicitly. Selective focus sets up a hierarchy, forcing us to see certain objects in an image as more or less important.

Photographic styling
Photography for advertising combines sophisticated styling and retouching techniques, in addition to the photography itself. Top specialists who shoot nothing but cars are able to use lighting, camera angle, and other techniques to bring out the subtleties of form that make a particular model—such as this Jeep Patriot—look its best, *and* reflect the values of the brand.

It should go without saying that the content and style of images should reflect the brand: if your car is supposed to be luxurious and roomy, the photos shouldn't make it look cheap and small. If your service is meant to appeal to a certain class of person, the models in the ads should really exude the attributes of that class.

When brands cross borders, brand managers must re-evaluate the visuals, especially those showing people. Ads are frequently reshot in each country so the models depicted don't look "foreign." This isn't prompted by racism; it is a realistic adaptation to audience response. It is human nature for customers in, say, Thailand to relate to different "types" than customers in Poland. A diverse group that is attractive to a multicultural market like the UK or the US will seem irrelevant to customers in places with more homogeneous populations.

Style is as important as content. The UK cell-phone company Orange used strong black-and-white images in the 1990s to differentiate its brand by giving it a cool realism. When the brand expanded from the UK to countries like Slovakia and Israel, its image was reconceived using color photography, as it was judged that black-and-white create the wrong impression in those markets.

Illustration

In some countries, like the US, illustration in advertising has a long tradition of wit and sophistication. In other markets, however, hand-drawn art may be seen as a poor substitute for slick photography. Of course, the style of illustration will have a huge effect on perception in any market, so all decisions about illustrative style must be approached carefully to ensure that customers will respond in the right way. When an artist with a readily identifiable style or subject matter is hired to illustrate a campaign, the brand is effectively getting an endorsement by association with that artist's personal brand. Nearly everyone is familiar, for example, with Andy Warhol's famous illustration for Absolut Vodka.

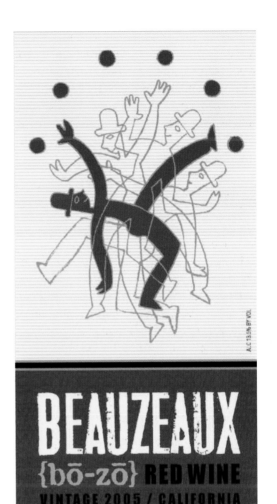

Illustrative styling

Before photo reproduction became as technically advanced as it is today, advertising relied on illustration to portray the brand in the desired light. This 1940s ad for Jeep uses compositions that would have been extremely hard to capture on camera at the time. Audiences were accustomed to illustration, so the ads were seen as modern and exciting.

Nowadays, illustration is often used to achieve a "retro" effect, as with the changing icon of Dutch Boy paints or the label for Diageo's Beauzeaux wine. For these brands, the illustration style emphasizes the traditional values of the product.

| 1907 | 1917 | 1927 | 1937 | 1947 | 1957 | 1967 | 1977 | 1987 to present |

Graphic motifs

One of the weapons graphic designers use to support the wholeness and harmony of a visual identity is the addition of an extra graphic motif. A frame, an area of color, or an unusual layout grid can all work to boost recognition and reinforce the memory of that brand. The right graphic motif can transfer well to environmental design and packaging.

When Penguin books introduced their now-famous line of quality paperbacks in the 1930s, a simple, modernist cover design, with broad bands of color surrounding the title, was adopted. Originally, different colors were used for different genres, but this soon proved too complex for customers to remember, and Penguin settled on orange as its trademark shade. Even today, after a myriad variations through the intervening years, Penguin covers have a recognizable quality thanks to the style of their designs.

National Geographic magazine displays perhaps the most famous example of using a frame as an identity element. The yellow rectangle is versatile enough to function not only as a design element, but also as a logo, and in signage. The familiar "Golden Arches" of the McDonald's logo began as an architectural element in a handful of roadside drive-in restaurants in California. The company later discovered that these arches—which, seen from an angle down the road, form a letter M—were a more recognizable feature to customers than the clown mascot or any other visual device. When Interbrand developed a new identity for the Mini, the frame became an integral part of the brand image. It was used on billboards, brochures, web pages, and as an architectural element in showrooms.

The use of a graphic element in a retail environment, what Interbrand likes to call a "supersign," can create a powerful visual mnemonic for the brand in a cluttered shopping area, especially at street level, as well as making an otherwise generic-looking space something more memorable.

MAKING THE
INVISIBLE VISIBLE
the fight against
lung cancer

Hello Kitty

Hello Kitty is different from Disney and popular cartoon characters in one key way: she does not have a pre-determined personality. As an instantly recognizable graphic motif, Hello Kitty provides a strong visual reinforcement of the brand that can be applied across a vast range of products and places without dissonance. And as she has developed over the decades, Hello Kitty has become something of an icon.

Left: Making the Invisible Visible: The Fight against Lung Cancer campaign
The identity created by Siegel+Gale for this campaign uses an iconic rendering of a balloon to highlight the negative space, literally making "visible" that which has previously been "invisible," as well as conveying, at another level, how many people are absent because of lung cancer.

Sound, smell, taste, touch

We absorb almost all the information we need in our daily lives through our eyes. This has been doubly true since the development of writing; and yet, even though vision is our primary sense, we use our other senses more often than we realize. Hunters do best when they can rely on their eyes, but they are able to track prey by sound and even by scent if necessary.

Even though we're often unaware of it, our other senses contribute a significant amount of extra information and experience to our everyday lives. As Martin Lindstrom demonstrates in his book *Brand Sense*, customers respond powerfully to brands that engage all of the senses.

Studies have proven something that bakers and chocolate-makers have always known: a strong, pleasant scent attracts people and encourages them to buy. The same is true of music, which is why shopping centers usually have some playing in the background. Music and sound can be integrated into brand experiences through arenas other than retail environments. Websites, radio, and TV advertising, even the noises emitted by a product itself, all can and should be designed to highlight a brand aurally. For example, T-Mobile has a five-note "sonic logo" that is used as a sign-off in commercials and as a default ringtone on the network's cell phones.

Good brands consider the oral as well as the aural. Some shops provide generic candy for customers, placing a bowl of it on their counter. Clever brand managers choose candy that matches the colors of the brand, in a custom wrapper with a logo. Really clever brand managers will make sure the flavor evokes the right associations as well: not too sweet, too tart, or too fruity; the right amount of playfulness or seriousness; the right degree of femininity or masculinity. Just thinking about what flavor best matches the brand personality can be a useful exercise for brand managers.

For food and drink products the flavor is all-important. But in addition to simply tasting good, the particular tastes of a given market can affect how a product is formulated to heighten the brand image.

International Flavor and Fragrance, established in the 1830s as a merchant in herbs, spices, and essential oils, now specializes in developing scents and taste experiences. In 2006 they created a "brandscent" for Samsung Experience Stores around the world (in partnership with branding agency Lippincott Mercer). The smell of the store is carefully crafted to match the brand identity, often without the customer being aware of it.

Touch is important too. In product design, the choice of plastics and other materials used in sporting goods, electronic devices, packaging, and a myriad other elements takes into account the feel of the material as well as the look, since both are integral to the brand image. Is it rugged? Gentle? Sleek? Flimsy? Is it something to be used quickly and put down, or lovingly held and enjoyed? Again, thinking about these issues can be helpful in identifying the essence of a brand.

All of our senses contribute to the impressions we form of the world around us. Branding professionals should take advantage of this and consider the other senses in designing every aspect of the brand experience: product, packaging, advertising, and retail environments. Customers certainly will, and their actions will be based on their sensory impressions.

Below: Local flavor
In Japan, Nestlé's KitKat is produced in a wide variety of exquisite flavors, such as green tea, banana, and cherry blossom, that are tailored to the tastes of local customers. The flavors help define the brand experience.

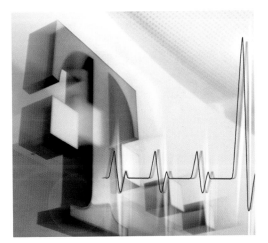

Left: The audible logo
Developed by Interbrand. One of the cleverest pieces of sensory branding is T-Mobile's distinctive sound signature, a rapid trill of five notes that serves equally well as the sign-off for TV commercials and as a ringtone for millions of customers. Every time someone's cell phone rings in a public place, it reinforces the brand's jingle.

Packaging

As we have seen, package design can often provide the whole reason for a brand to exist. In spite of this, the package is just one of several tools in the brand-building tool kit. Some products simply can't be sold unpackaged, so they are put in bags, boxes, bottles, jars, cans, cartons, or tied to a board or holder of some kind. Packaging can accomplish several functions. It can:

• communicate brand identity (achieved by differentiating a product from its competitors, telling a story, conveying an image of value, and making an emotional impression);
• attract attention in a busy retail space (the package serves as sign and advertisement);
• position a product within a certain category or price range;
• perform a useful function, even supplanting the product itself in importance (the package serves as container and protector, and carries instructions for use and information on nutrition, health, and safety); and
• fulfill some corollary function (the package can serve as souvenir merchandise—think of jam jars printed with "collectible" designs, giving them a residual branding value long after the contents have been used up—or as storage containers, like the plastic buckets that some LEGO bricks are sold in).

The Coca-Cola bottle
The famous contour of the Coca-Cola bottle is an integral part of its identity. It has evolved over time in a way that makes it memorable and widely recognized. This recognition allows the brand to take new liberties with the design, such as the "M5" promotion during 2005, in which independent designers created a series of refreshingly edgy, offbeat designs to promote Coca-Cola in night-clubs and alternative venues.

1899-1902   1900–1916   1915   1957   1961   1991   1994

All of these are achieved through the astute use of design. Conveying the brand message is the single most important task, but the others must not be neglected.

The design of the package must reflect the qualities associated with the brand. Is it fancy? Cheap? For people who care a lot about their clothes? For people with no time to worry about clothes? Is it the one my mother used? And most important of all, is it the one I want to use?

The desire to make the strongest brand statement possible sometimes leads to goods being unnecessarily overpackaged. As customers become more aware of and concerned with the impact of human activity on the environment, some brands are touting their use of postconsumer recycled packaging, packaging that is easily biodegradable, or offering goods with minimal packaging, or none at all.

For many fast-moving consumer goods (the products in your supermarket), the package is virtually the only brand experience the customer has between the time the buying decision is made and the time the product is used up. While the quality of my laundry detergent is important (how clean are my clothes, how nice do they smell?), the thing customers are going to remember most of all is the package: that's what they'll look for next time they buy detergent.

Ensuring standout
The same manufacturer may produce a number of different generic or house brands that are all offered as commodities, even packaged in identical bottles. Unless they make an effort to be different, brands in this category will be lost. Here, only Hebrew National stands out, because it is an extension of a popular hot-dog brand.

Convention vs. differentiation
Packaging for common items usually follows design conventions that have evolved over many decades. Looking at the example of spaghetti, we see a combination of practical considerations, such as the shape of the packet, and more abstract conventions, such as the frequent use of the color blue. Generic and house brands tend to follow the leaders. How can a brand stand out and differentiate itself, while still relying on conventions to guarantee its appeal? How can a brand in a crowded market use design strategy to rise above the level of a commodity?

Merchandise, environments, and signage

The word merchandise has two meanings: creating things to sell, and arranging those things in a shop in such a way as to maximize sales. At the mention of *Star Wars* the first meaning becomes clear through the toys and video games, clothing, interior decor, and all manner of goods based on its galaxy of exotic characters. An old story has it that George Lucas agreed to forego his fee for the first *Star Wars* movie, but kept the rights to make and sell merchandise, which wasn't considered valuable in the 1970s. The rest is marketing history.

Merchandising involves the art of positioning things in a retail environment to encourage customers to buy as much as possible. A clothing shop might display certain items together according to color, for example, to maximize their appeal to customers. Department stores dress mannequins in coordinated outfits to suggest additional purchases. Impulse items are placed at the checkout counter. In supermarkets, brands vie to get shelf space at eye level; brands displayed near the floor tend to be cheaper, or generic staples that sell automatically. Brands that lose the struggle for eye-level shelf space often die as shoppers forget them.

When customers walk into a shop, showroom, trade-fair booth, service center, or corporate headquarters, they are physically entering a brand space. The experience this environment presents needs to be consistent with the rest of the brand identity and image. It does not necessarily identical, but integrated in a coherent fashion.

Environmental signage
Signage serves not only as a guide and orientation for visitors, but also as a presentation of brand identity. Its whole design—the forms and colors, as well as how it is crafted—embodies the brand and imparts an impression of the company's values.

The best environment designs find appropriate ways to give customers the thrill of discovery, to come across as authentic, and to echo the brand's insights and ideas, while maintaining a visual and sensory link to the brand identity. This can be accomplished through obvious devices such as large wall decorations and custom-built furnishings, as well as through subtler means such as lighting, and even special scents wafted into a space. Customers of Singapore Airlines always remark on how good the planes smell. That scent is a deliberate part of the brand.

Signs are a key element in any environment. They establish orientation, impart information, and help customers navigate a space. Through clever use of color, typography, and form, the best signs also impart a sense of the brand's personality. Good signage makes the whole environment better. Poor or generic signage leaves the visitor uncertain or lost, and drags the whole brand experience down.

Signs often try to employ "universal" symbols rather than words. In principle this is a fine impulse, but symbols can be ambiguous, and culture-specific. Sometimes it is better to use six common languages rather than one unintelligible icon.

Branded environments
The polished, hi-tech interiors of Apple's retail stores emphasize the innovations that make the brand famous, and provide a friendly, helpful environment for customers to interact with the support staff, thus furthering the brand's reputation for ease of use.

Price positioning

How much an item costs is as much a part of its brand and positioning as its design and advertising. Price is perhaps the least glamorous element of branding, but it is one of the most crucial because it's the price that really indicates what strength a brand has.

A brand is what allows a product to rise above "parity" pricing and commodity status; to be sold for more than an equivalent product that lacks the brand. If a customer is considering only the price when buying a product, then the item is a commodity. If a customer is buying because of other factors—design, quality, features, ease of use, glamour, pleasant associations, a recommendation, personal memories— and is willing to pay more because of them, then the brand is working. The more a seller can charge, and still have customers clamoring for the product, the stronger the economic value of the brand.

Price setting is often the domain of corporate marketing departments. This is because pricing is widely recognized as an integral part of a brand strategy. Firms don't just charge what they need to recover costs of production, nor do they charge "whatever they can get for it," although both of those tendencies are strong. In ideal circumstances, the price is set to take into consideration factors such as how the price affects brand perception, where the price will position the product in relation to its competitors, and what pressures will develop on the price as the market matures.

What effect does price have on how a brand is perceived? In *A New Brand World*, Scott Bedbury describes the so-called "Marlboro Friday," the day in 1993 when the tobacco giant Philip Morris announced it would have to slash the price of its world-famous Marlboro cigarettes in order to compete against lesser brands. This decision sent shock waves through the marketing world, since it represented a blunt admission that the Marlboro brand had little value. The new pricing strategy seemed to undermine the rationale for all brands.

The problem with Marlboro, Bedbury explains, was that the product itself wasn't innovative enough to distinguish it from competing cigarettes. There was nothing in the user experience to support the brand image that Philip Morris had spent millions promoting worldwide. Stripped of its brand, the product appeared to have no perceived extra value.

Of course, cigarettes suffer from other issues, such as enormous lawsuits, declining sales, loss of social standing, and so on. Brands such as Marlboro might have been in trouble anyway. But the lesson is that price is an excellent bellwether of brand strength; the canary in a coal mine that signals imminent disaster. When marketers are forced to cut the price of any premium item, whether cigarettes, cell phones, hair coloring, or brokerage services, the demise of the brand cannot be far off.

Pricing
Banned in many countries from other forms of advertising, cigarette brands are allowed to do little more than state their prices. Price jockeying is something all brands do, though usually in more subtle fashion, and complemented by other techniques.

CAMEL
PLEASURE TO BURN

$5.50

SPECIAL OFFER INCLUDING TAX

SALEM

SURGEON GENERAL'S WARNING: Quitting Smoking Now Greatly Reduces Serious Risks to Your Health.

SALEM

SPECIAL PRICE

$5.55

SPECIAL OFFER INCLUDING TAX

Winston NO BULL

SURGEON GENERAL'S WARNING: Smoking By Pregnant Women May Result In Fetal Injury, Premature Birth, And Low Birth Weight.

No additives in our tobacco does **NOT** mean a safer cigarette.

SPECIAL $5.50

SPECIAL OFFER

Advertising

For most of the twentieth century, advertising *was* branding. It is still a critical tool for shaping how brands are perceived. James B. Twitchell, in *Twenty Ads that Shook the World*, describes the Absolut vodka campaign that began in the 1980s, and the effect those ads had on the world's ideas about vodka. The clear, almost flavorless spirit went from being an undistinguished, fairly generic form of alcohol to one of the most desirable, glamourous, and differentiated drink categories, practically overnight.

Although he understates the role of product quality (Absolut is purer than other vodkas, and distilled by a slightly different process from most other brands), Twitchell rightly attributes the brand's success to its triumph in advertising and packaging.

Print

Brands that are advertised in print media (such as magazines and newspapers) can make certain assumptions about the people seeing the ads. With the long-term trend away from general-interest publications and toward niche titles, it is possible to focus an ad very carefully on a small group of people with a high degree of interest in one subject. For example, a maker of kayaks can place an ad in *Sea Kayaker* magazine (or one of several competing titles) to reach precisely the sort of people who might react to the ad by buying a kayak in the near future.

What isn't necessarily known is how much time each reader spends looking at an ad, or whether seeing an ad results in the reader buying a product soon, or having a more favorable opinion of the brand in the future. For this reason, advertisers are constantly testing audiences to see if they have noticed particular ads, and if so, what their impression of the brand was.

As well as trying to reach a particular market segment, each brand forms an association with the brand of the magazine or newspaper in which the ad appears: Canon advertises its cameras in *National Geographic* magazine; Jack Daniels advertises in *Playboy*; Macy's in *The New York Times*. The reputation of each title affects how readers perceive the brands in the ads too.

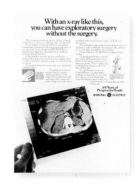

Left: Focused advertising
Print advertising need not
be limited to publications.
Getting right to the heart of
their target market, breweries
supply pubs with beer mats
advertising their beers.

**Above: Consistency
of message**
The continued strength
of GE's brand, despite
extraordinary diversification
and extension, is due partly
to the idea of inventing
everything. Much of GE's
advertising is based simply
on introducing revolutionary
products to the world. This
message has remained
consistent in its magazine
campaigns for over a century.

On-air advertising
The power of broadcast media to reach vast captive audiences has been well known since WWII, when brands like Ivory sponsored on-air game and talk shows. Later, brands like Xerox used TV to tell engaging stories about their products. The increasing cinematographic sophistication of TV spots, such as these for KitKat from Japan in the 1980s (left) and 2000s (right), can be a delight to deconstruct, especially when analyzing how they reinforce the brand message.

Broadcast

Once upon a time, advertising on TV was the best way to guarantee big success for your brand. It was expensive, but you could reach millions of potential customers in 30 seconds, with a powerfully persuasive message. The aura of the tube was such that any brand seen on TV gained instant cachet as a market leader.

Those days are gone: for one thing, alternatives such as the web compete for attention, and for another, people don't watch TV like they used to. They watch cable or satellite "on demand." They record programs and skip the commercials. They click on streaming web videos. They buy their favorite shows on DVD.

As TV has become more fractured, it has followed the trend in magazines toward niche audiences, allowing brands to focus on more specific groups of viewers. TV advertising—whether the classic 30-second spot or the 30-minute infomercial—is certainly not about to disappear.

Outdoor

There is something at once appalling and appealing about a large billboard. The billboard is a primitive medium, passive and indiscriminate, and yet these gigantic posters, aspiring on some level to public art, a space-age legacy of ancient cave paintings, inevitably inspire awe and command our attention. The cleverest billboards take into account the context of their placement. Whether in a London tube station or on a Californian freeway, they can make sly inferences about the people looking at them, and say something knowing about how the brands they hawk can fit into the lifestyles of their viewers.

Direct mail

Ever since David Ogilvy proved the efficacy of direct mail, with penny postcards advertising a local hotel, our mailboxes (and more recently our e-mail inboxes) have been flooded with junk mail. Direct mail takes advantage of the fact that most of us still think of our mailboxes as a personal space through which our friends and families

communicate with us. We tend to be receptive to any message arriving there. Mailers and spammers consider even tiny response rates successful.

Perhaps surprisingly, direct mail will work for almost any brand. Although most "junk mail" is perceived as common, if the item being mailed is fancy enough, and sent to the right people, it can succeed at selling luxury items. Some direct-mail pieces are elaborate and expensive, and very effective.

Web

Web advertising, which started out with simple banners, is now run by highly sophisticated software that conjures a miniature, full-featured website within the banner itself. Web advertising not only plays video and animation, interacts with viewers, provides customized content, and gathers information about viewers, it also bills advertisers based on such things as how many telephone inquiries or purchases result from the ad.

Large-scale advertising
When the youth-oriented clothing retailer Abercrombie & Fitch renovated its midtown Manhattan store, it covered the building with this gigantic billboard. Advances in technology have made the production of enormous outdoor images more common, but their scale still has the power to draw attention, if not to shock.

Web advertising offers extraordinary opportunities for creating fuller brand experiences. The most effective come from combining the web with another medium— or the product itself—to drive viewers in a happy circle from web to store to product and back to web for follow-up that may include customer care or a better way to use the product.

Wearable

For some reason, people seem to enjoy wearing logos on their T-shirts, caps, and jackets. They act as free, walking billboards for the logos' owners, on top of generating sales revenue for them.

Many writers have explored the sociology from the wearer's side, looking at how having a logo emblazoned on your chest/ back/head gives you a sense of belonging, an association with a glamourous brand, or a way to identify yourself through your own conspicuous consumption.

What fewer people have looked at is how wearable advertising affects brands. Seeing an unwashed slob in an Emporio Armani shirt doesn't do much to raise the perception of that brand. Shouldn't Armani be more careful about who they sell their shirts to? In fact, fashion brands do take care by setting the retail price of the clothing item at a level that's meant to function selectively. Non-clothing brands, from Budweiser to T-Mobile to Caterpillar, have less control because they're more likely to be giving the items away.

Publicity and public relations

If advertising is the visible face of a brand, then the craft known around the world as "PR" is the invisible one.

Since the early days of PR, when Edward Bernays succeeded in breaking the age-old taboo against women smoking in public by turning New York's famous Easter Parade into a mile-long demonstration of "women's liberation," with one glamourous woman after another puffing happily away in the spring sunshine, the PR business has aimed at what Bernays liked to call "engineering consent" on behalf of its clients.

PR often works closely with the news media, "planting" favorable stories in newspapers and on TV. Communication is generally much more effective if it is seen to come from an "impartial" source, such as a news broadcaster, rather than through a blatantly commercial message. However, as consumers become more savvy, and more cynical, about the media, they are often able to see through this ruse and recognize planted stories for what they are.

Many times the tactic is not to promote a brand overtly, but to sway public opinion in order to leave people more receptive to commercial messages that may follow. For example, if a PR firm can persuade news channels to increase their coverage of events that raise public anxiety, the public may respond by supporting one of the PR firm's clients, which may be a security firm, a maker of antidepressant drugs, or a right-wing politician.

While the methods of PR are varied, the goal is the same: to get something to happen, to get people to agree that it is good, and to leave people unaware of how much their point of view is being influenced by someone else. PR operations like to stay unseen because a large part of their effectiveness comes from the public not fully grasping that their opinions are being manipulated.

In *The Fall of Advertising and the Rise of PR*, Al and Laura Ries advance the argument that while advertising was once a powerful tool for building brands, nowadays publicity is more efficient and effective for generating new interest in a product, with advertising relegated to the role of maintaining a brand that is already established.

In the service of consumer brands, PR is generally used to achieve nothing more sinister than increased sales. Two of the more frequent activities of PR include setting up and financially backing a promotional event, and sponsoring a sportsperson or sports event. In both cases, the goal is to gain a visible presence with a relatively small audience that has a common interest, and to promote the client's brand by associating it with that athlete or event. The value of the sponsorship or event is then extended through use of the resulting images in advertising.

Event sponsorship
As part of an event sponsorship, Target, the department store, used a "pop-up" temporary store location to publicize its efforts to fight against breast cancer.

Alternative marketing

Buzz campaign, word of mouth, viral marketing ... Whatever the jargon, it all amounts to the same thing—trying to reach customers in spite of their increasing immunity to the many commercial images, messages, and sales pitches they receive every day. The many methods include tactics like social networking, blogging, podcasting, video sharing, product placement, and product integration, and new methods will undoubtedly be added to this list.

In *Purple Cow* marketing guru Seth Godin writes, "The traditional approaches are now obsolete... One hundred years of marketing thought are gone. Alternative approaches aren't a novelty—they are all we've got left." Though Godin admits he may be guilty of a little hyperbole, his point that today's customers frequently ignore advertising and other traditional marketing methods is valid. To have any chance of succeeding, marketers must toss out the old rules and find stealthier ways of getting through.

Consumers have become much more savvy about the techniques used to sell things. Often the most convincing motivation to buy something comes from a friend or colleague. Many marketers now try to encourage customers to communicate with their friends about a new product. They focus their efforts not on marketing to the masses, but on swaying a handful of influential "early adopters" who will then recommend the product to others.

On the one hand, this is somewhat insidious—a way of sneaking a commercial pitch into personal interactions that ought to be free of such pandering. On the other hand, who hasn't discussed a product or service with a friend or colleague in the past week, while shopping together, watching TV, chatting, or just hanging out? The purpose of so-called word-of-mouth or viral marketing is simply to channel in a particular direction those discussions about products that are taking place naturally.

7301
Interlock Running Short

NEW!

NEW!

Virtual-world branding
American Apparel, a retail chain with a rebellious, sexy image, was one of the first real-world brands to open a shop in *Second Life*, the online virtual world. For a few pennies customers can buy digital copies of real-life clothing for their avatars (online characters). This doesn't generate much income for American Apparel, but it does get the brand noticed and talked about.

Like PR, alternative marketing techniques work best when the audience isn't overtly aware of them. Marketers who use them rely heavily on "opinion leaders" to spread the word among their circle of acquaintances. They may ply visitors at a party or nightclub with free samples of their product, or give luxury goods to celebrities for them to show off in public. While the marketing purpose of such actions cannot be hidden, it is made to appear incidental, almost natural.

Product placement, by which a brand-name item is prominently visible in a movie or television program, is nothing new. Audiences generally realize that when the camera lingers on a logo for a few seconds, it is not by chance—money has changed hands. More recently, this has evolved into what is called product integration: an entire episode or scene is written around the sponsor's product, with characters discussing it and the plot perhaps being resolved through it. The technique actually dates to the 1940s, when De Beers asked Hollywood screen-writers to portray their leading men buying diamond engagement rings. Diamonds became ingrained in the public mind as a symbol of lasting love, to the enormous benefit of the diamond-trading cartel.

A more recent trend is "advergaming;" giving brands a central role in a video game or online interactive environment. Brands like Nissan and American Apparel were among the first to open virtual showrooms and stores in the popular online world *Second Life*. How these alternative channels become integrated with the rest of the brand relationship remains to be seen.

++ minivacant in shanghai

Pop-up shops
Vacant is one of several firms specializing in what are known as pop-up shops. These appear for just a few hours or days to promote a brand, guerrilla-style, in a prime location that would be too expensive for a permanent presence. In Shanghai, a stretch-limousine version of the Mini enthralled the public; in San Francisco, various limited-edition sneakers and other exclusive products designed by artists were sold in a shop-front location. Such events lend the brands a hip, streetwise cachet.

Ambassadors and internal branding

For service brands, the people who interact directly with customers are the key to building the right brand experience. People are the "fifth P" (after product, place, promotion, and price; see page 26) that determines the line between products and services. A product, broadly defined, is anything that doesn't require an immediate human element for its delivery: a can of soup, a computer, a CD. If it needs a human to deliver it—a restaurant meal, a parcel, the news report, or a concert—it's a service.

How a brand's people communicate with clients and fulfill customer expectations, as well as how they are trained, dressed, groomed, and rewarded for their work, is crucial. It is difficult to overstate the importance of the human element of a brand, especially a service brand.

Such brand "ambassadors" can be found in many places. They attend to passengers on planes, trains, and bus lines. They greet customers at the entrance to a store. They work as bank tellers and as counter staff at shipping offices. They visit places where prospective customers can be approached for a few minutes, such as trade fairs and shopping centers, but also less likely places such as city parks and nightclubs.

Ambassadors for special product promotions are often dressed in creative outfits that emphasize key visual elements of the brand in a way designed to catch attention. Because they are worn for relatively short periods, and during special events, they can afford to look unusual or even outrageous. The everyday uniforms of service personnel, on the other hand, tend to be more conservative and need to take comfort and mobility into account. It is important that the brand is recognizable to customers, and that they perceive the person to be a dependable part of the brand—perhaps even a figure of authority.

But it takes more than the appropriate clothes to make a person truly represent their company's brand. They also need to assume the proper outlook, the proper talk, the proper smile, the proper knowledge to answer questions and solve customers' problems. All of this is accomplished through personnel training, an area that was once the sole domain of corporate Human Resources departments, but is now coming more and more under the oversight of branding and marketing departments.

Aside from training employees in how to talk, walk, and respond to customers' needs, companies need to communicate regularly with employees, to keep them abreast of news that affects the company, and to provide them with the latest insights and knowledge on how their work benefits the brand. As the company gets larger, the importance of internal communication grows. It is not hard for a company of 50 people to get together and hear their boss give a talk. For a global company of thousands, this is physically impossible. One way is for top managers to talk with middle managers, and middle managers to talk to the rank and file. Another way is to share information via written communication such as internal newsletters, e-mail, and intranets.

Each of these methods has its drawbacks, but a savvy brand manager will take the time to employ them to their full advantage, encouraging communication to ensure that every employee understands the way his or her job, however routine or unglamourous, has some impact on customer experience, and therefore on the brand.

Celebrity ambassadors
The Swedish clothing retailer H&M launched its first store in Shanghai in 2007 with a concert by the Australian singer Kylie Minogue, one of many celebrities who model for H&M. The concert included a Chinese all-girls' choir singing Minogue's songs.

Customer support

Customer experience management, service, or care: whatever the name, it's about the human contact between a company and its customers.

There is an old business truism: failure to provide satisfactory customer support (also called customer service) is the single biggest reason brands lose their hard-won customers. I once raved enthusiastically to a friend about an airline my wife and I frequently flew with. "Oh yeah?" said my friend. "Wait until they lose your baggage." I thought he was being unduly pessimistic, until one holiday the inevitable happened: my wife got off her plane minus two suitcases. The temporary loss wasn't so irksome—accidents do happen—but the airline's indifferent attitude made us furious. Everyone we spoke to passed us on to someone else, put us in touch with clueless cargo handlers, and generally made us feel as though it had been we and not the airline who had lost our bags. After three days, a driver showed up and dumped the bags unceremoniously—and minus a few of their contents—on our doorstep, in the middle of the night. We never got any apologies or follow-up of any sort from the airline. Needless to say, we booked our next flights with someone else.

Customer care is much more important for a service than a product. Most people need to visit their bank at least occasionally to speak to a live person. Not many people feel the urge to visit the makers of their toothpaste or baked beans.

Good customer support involves more than reacting well to a routine problem like a lost suitcase. The term "customer care" is apt: when customer care is good, employees care about their customers. They do a little extra to make sure they're satisfied. They treat them well. They exceed what the customer expected; sometimes by a lot. In *Positively Outrageous Service*, T. Scott Gross offers countless anecdotes about how customers were looked after in outrageously wonderful ways.

Providing a level of customer service that exceeds expectations is the best way to generate "buzz" and get people talking about a brand. Smart brands will fall over themselves to impress their most influential users—especially the early adopters who try out a new product or service before it becomes really popular—knowing that those users will then spread the word among the rest of the population, effectively doing word-of-mouth advertising on the company's behalf.

In *Purple Cow*, Seth Godin likens remarkable brands to viruses. Those who catch one early "sneeze" it around to everyone else. Godin identifies remarkable brands not only as innovative, but also as providing superior customer service, which makes happy users into passionate true believers.

It's hard to overstate how important customer service is to a brand. It could be said that customer service is more critical to a brand's success than its ideas, its identity, or its advertising and publicity.

Earning customer loyalty
No one gets too passionate about a logo, but the world is full of brands that have legions of cult followers, and their secret ingredient is always superior customer support.

Fast-moving consumer goods

The supermarket is a metaphor for our consumer society; it is the place we go to learn about, select, and buy food and drink, detergent, shampoo, toothpaste, cough medicine and cigarettes, magazines, sweets, and dozens of other things we don't even really need. These are consumer products, also known in the ad business as FMCGs, or fast-moving consumer goods.

In the 1990s, one of the explanations given for the collapse of Soviet communism was the State's inability to provide its citizens with the attractive consumer products that all people supposedly crave. While this may have been an overstatement by Westerners, it is generally true that people like to buy branded goods. Buying brands gets you a place in an idealized world and satisfies the desire aroused by brands' advertising. Whether we like it or not, this is a fact of life.

Food and drink

Buying food was once a bit of a gamble; it was hard to know if what you were getting was fresh, or of the right measure. When producers grasped that a reputation for quality and honesty was the surest way to success, they began to put their names on the goods they shipped so that customers could buy with confidence. These producers became the first brands. Their names were literally burned onto packing crates. Today, the branding of FMCGs has to function not only as an identifier, but also as an advertiser and customer-service provider.

Every society has its own conventions for food packaging, based on what marketers have determined customers respond to best. This is why so many packaged goods in the same category resemble one another. The look and feel of a package is called its "trade dress," and big brands have to expend a lot of effort in protecting the individuality of their trade dress from imitators to avoid confusing consumers.

Iconic design
Campbell's, the brand Andy Warhol turned into an icon in the 1960s, has successfully extended and updated its product lines and packaging, without losing any brand equity. The original design (the Campbell's can shown here), is still on store shelves alongside newer ones; it appeals mainly to consumers who remember the pop art it inspired.

Conventions naturally differ from one culture to another. In the US, instant coffee with a red label has caffeine, while a green label indicates decaffeinated. In Europe, it is usually the opposite. Conventions also change over time. Black used to be a forbidden color in food packaging, until someone realized that ice cream wrapped in black looks more expensive. The packaging of so-called premium foods now frequently uses black to denote luxury.

Package design for foods creates associations that give a branded product more value by telling a story, conjuring up romantic ideas about dining that the product hopes to fulfill. As Louis Cheskin (a prominent marketer, and one of the first to investigate how package design affects consumers) discovered in the 1950s, these associations, when carefully put together, enhance the brand image and increase sales.

For drinks, even more than food, the packaging and branding have to do the lion's share of the work. Most soft drinks are very cheap to mass-produce—basic ingredients are water, corn syrup, coloring, and a few drops of actual juice—and there is only so much a producer can do to differentiate one sugar water from another.

As consumers become more health conscious, the market for plain water is booming, matched by a boom in water brands. Evian, a well-known pioneer of the trend, has done a remarkable job of staying relevant as a brand in an increasingly crowded category.

Promoting product origin
As with most brands of mineral water, the origin is prominent in Fiji water's name. Its qualities—pure artesian source, unspoiled by human development—are underscored by the label design, and reinforced by advertising.

Personal-care and household products

Other categories of FMCGs are even more dependent on branding because their contents (being inedible) are often more mysterious. Who knows what their shampoo is really made of? Personal-care products often take advantage of positioning and lifestyle associations. "If you use this cream, you will be more glamourous," they seem to say. Proctor & Gamble's Ivory Lady (featured in the brand's first color ad, in *Cosmopolitan* in 1896) was a pioneering use of this strategy (see pages 72–3). In the twenty-first century, many products aim at the highest tier of Maslow's hierarchy of needs—the need for self-actualization—with an appeal that includes not only well-being, but also concern for the environment, and harmony with the natural world. (Maslow proposed his theory of human motivation, with the hierarchy of needs, in 1943.) The imagery of nature that is a mainstay of personal-care packaging has a soothing effect that counteracts our fears of artificial chemicals and their possible consequences.

Pharmaceuticals

The drug industry comes up with thousands of new products every year. All of them need names—unique, catchy names that can be pronounced and remembered. Along with the successes, such as Prozac and Viagra, are thousands that only pharmacists know. The imperatives of the drug business dictate that made-up names, generally with Greco-Latin roots, predominate. Unfortunately, such names tend to be abstract and difficult to remember.

Drugs packaging tends to adopt a generic look for prescription medicines that don't need to sell themselves off the shelf, and a bold, brightly colored look for those that do.

There is a third approach, used by many natural and herbal remedies, which is to opt for a gentler look, using finer typography and images of plants or people. Because of the volume of work and the highly specialized nature of pharmaceutical branding, some large branding agencies have separate operations, each devoted exclusively to a different "set" of clients.

Natural imagery
The imagery of nature is often used on household products, both to allay fears of dangerous chemicals, and to promote the idea of caring for the environment. The core values of Ecover—honesty and transparency—provided a starting point for the packaging of its household goods. The transparent bottle follows the idea that the product has nothing to hide, and with no paper label, all the materials used can be recycled together. Cif is promoted with a design and campaign that highlights the part it plays in addressing global environmental and social concerns.

Music, books, and film

The marketing of music, books, and film has to solve some inherent conflicts: the work is linear, and in the case of music, nonvisual, but it has to be sold using instantaneous visual impressions. The most successful marketing images have become icons of their times, like the cover of *Abbey Road* or a classic orange-and-white Penguin paperback. There are three ways to approach branding a work like this:

- promote the work itself, its genre, or its literary tradition;
- promote its author; or
- promote its publisher.

Musicians often cultivate a visual style that symbolizes their work. In the case of U2, for example, it is the stark black-and-white photography of Anton Corbijn. In the case of the Rolling Stones, it is the many variations of the tongue-and-lips symbol developed by John Pasche in 1972, and subsequently adopted by fans everywhere as a symbol not just of the Stones' music, but also of their rebellious attitude.

Consistent styling
U2's album covers are key ingredients of the band's image, using the stark, sometimes dreamy black-and-white photography of Anton Corbijn to capture the atmosphere of the band's music visually. When the band wanted to return to their earlier sound, they also returned to using Corbijn's pictures as the central focus of their album-cover art.

Penguin Books' logo is so widely known that while Terry Waite was a hostage in Lebanon, he was able to communicate to his captors that he wanted something to read by drawing a penguin. And he got what he wanted. In the 1930s Penguin set out to provide readers with good, cheap literature. They chose to convey these attributes through a distinctive cover design, developed by Eric Gill. The look of Penguin covers has, through many different styles, maintained the brand image of affordable quality for over 70 years.

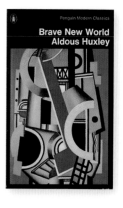

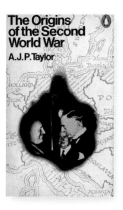

The Penguin brand has promised readers quality mass-market literature for over 70 years. The distinctive orange-and-white cover designs evolved into a diverse mix of visuals that still stand together, even though no single logo or motif binds them. The details of the penguin logo itself have also evolved, but the brand is still recognizable. Many covers, especially from the 1960s, are icons of their times.

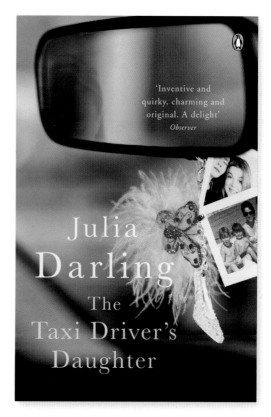

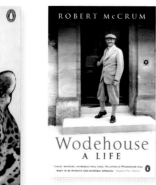

Durable goods

Cars, furniture, computers, appliances like washing machines or TVs, jewelry, sports equipment, and many other items fall under the category of what economists call durable goods—things that are meant to last. It's also fair to consider some business-to-business categories, such as construction equipment, under this rubric. What these items all have in common, from a branding perspective, is that because they represent a bigger purchase, customers tend to consider their options more deliberately, and choose more rationally than emotionally. However, that doesn't mean the brand isn't important. On the contrary, it is more important because more is at stake in creating the right perception of value.

Automobiles

The branding of cars is probably more scientific than that for any other item, simply because there is so much at stake. Cars are the second most expensive thing most people buy in their lives (after their house), and car companies stand to earn (or lose) billions of dollars a year depending on the success of their brand.

Clotaire Rapaille, the Swiss-American anthropologist and expert on brands, believes each culture has what he terms a "code" for the things they buy. The American code for automobiles, he says, is identity. Americans want to be known by what they drive. For them, a car is not just a useful gadget for getting from A to B; it is an expression of their selves.

Rapaille's ideas have been very influential on the design and styling of a generation of cars in North America. Why do enormous, inefficient Hummers sell so well? Americans like to feel dominant. When you drive one, you feel on top of the world.

Germans, on the other hand, identify cars with engineering. They like cars that are well made, fast, safe, and long-lasting. The slogan *Vorsprung durch Technik*—which, loosely translated, means "progress through technology"—resonates with a European customer, but not an American one.

In Rapaille's thinking, a specific car can also have its own code. For example, in Americans' minds, Jeep is associated with the idea of a horse. It'll go anywhere. Rapaille recommended changing the Jeep's headlights from square to round to reinforce this association, and American advertising successfully pushed the idea of a Jeep as a "go-anywhere" vehicle. In Europe, on the other hand, Jeeps have a close cultural association with liberation. Chrysler's marketing of Jeeps in France and Germany played up the symbolism of freedom.

Car companies seem to spend the lion's share of their energy staying up-to-date, constantly revising styling, adding options, and tweaking performance. Nevertheless, when it comes to branding, many automakers strive for a traditional look. This can be seen in cars' logos, some of which date back nearly a century. A surprising number of car logos incorporate some kind of heraldic symbolism.

LARAKI

Mercedes-Benz

KIA

VOLVO

Ford

TOYOTA

HONDA

CHRYSLER

CHRYSLER

RENAULT

JAGUAR

Auto branding
Most logos for automobile
brands are either circular,
winged, or feature a fast
animal. The implications
are obvious.

AUDI

Jeep

Cadillac.

Conveying worth

Design by Paprika. Birks, a leading North-American luxury jewelry brand, represents a heritage of trust, quality, and courteous service. For this bag Paprika created two Pantone colors specifically for Birks' use in order to give the bag a high-end and unique finish. In addition, a number of high-quality finishing processes were used, including foil blocking, lamination, and the use of matching-colored metal eyelets to hold in the ribbon and cord handles.

Many car manufacturers give their advertising agencies and graphic designers very precise instructions regarding how to depict their cars in ads, web pages, brochures, and PR materials. The brand image depends on the car being perceived in a certain way, so things like the angle of photography are carefully specified. This ensures that the car won't look too long or too short, too fat or too small. Of course, most drivers want the actual experience of driving a vehicle before they buy it, but the marketing materials can get a buyer interested and put them in the desired frame of mind before they open the door and sit behind the wheel.

Computers and electronics

The marketing of computers and consumer electronics has gone through a similar development to the marketing of soap (see pages 72–3), but in much less time—three decades as opposed to more than ten.

When computers and other advanced electronics were first introduced as consumer goods, around 1970, magazine ads touted basic capabilities. "This gadget can do this." (As they were a novelty, this was presumably reason enough to want to buy them.) Later ads gave the message, "*You* can do this because this gadget can do this." (One step up the ladder, from feature to benefit.) Later still, the message became "Your life/work/fun will be fantastic if you buy this gadget." (The final stage in the hierarchy of needs: self-actualization.)

Even after establishing a lifestyle (or workstyle) benefit, advertising for computers and electronics still emphasizes technical specifications, whereas the advertising for soaps rests firmly with lifestyle. Presumably, this is because the audience for these devices cares more about their technical capabilities than the audience for soap cares about its constituents.

Luxury goods, fragrances, and sporting goods

Building a luxury brand is the ultimate exercise in positioning. A luxury product needs to be more than just top-quality and well designed. It needs to be offered in the right venue, by the right sort of person, for the right price, which means high enough to be exclusive.

The trick of branding a plentiful commodity such as diamonds—convincing people to pay a high price for a rock of no particular rarity or worth, and then to attach sentimental value to it—surely qualifies as one of the greatest positioning successes of all time. Starting in the 1940s, De Beers and its partners managed to convince Hollywood screenwriters to write scenes into their movies in which leading men chose a diamond engagement ring for their leading ladies, cementing the association between diamonds and romantic commitment in the public mind. Strangely though, it is only in the twenty-first century that diamond retailers such as Swarovsky and Zales have begun to build their own brands. And, as awareness of so-called conflict diamonds has made buyers more concerned about who profits from the diamond trade, origin branding for diamonds is also becoming important, with "safe" countries like Canada etching miniature logos on the sides of diamonds they export.

Clothing and footwear

Few areas are as brand-conscious as the world of fashion. The label on a garment sometimes seems to be worth more than the garment itself. Fashion is, in many ways, an epitome of branding and a paradox. Fashion can be seen as a pinnacle of branding because it is not just about style, materials, tailoring, and price; it is also about presenting an image and making a social statement. It relies on the belief that the clothes *do* make the man (or woman). It is about social positioning and the expression of a personal brand. You are what you wear. A fashion brand is usually closely tied to the personal brand of a fashion designer. Customers are aware that they are loyal to a brand because they feel an affinity with the designer's values.

Fashion, more than any other category, also thrives on its products rapidly becoming obsolete, literally going out of fashion. This constant hunger for something new is fine for fashion, but has spread to many other areas of popular culture (including mobile phones and MP3 players), not always to good effect.

Tools and construction

Business-to-business (B2B) categories need to convey the brand insights that are particularly relevant to their category, and perhaps more importantly, to reassure their customers that their buying decision will stand the test of time. With many so-called B2B purchases, the buyer will not be the end user, except perhaps occasionally. He or she is making a decision on behalf of a contractor, who is working for a developer, who will hand the final product over to its real users. Therefore, the buyer has less at stake personally, but more at stake professionally. Many B2B brands know this instinctively, but don't always succeed in mastering the brand messages needed to convey this insight.

One brand that has mastered it is Caterpillar, a maker of heavy construction equipment. The brand has been successfully extended into high-quality work boots, drawing on the insight of durability while reinforcing the brand on a personal level.

CATERPILLAR®

TODAY'S WORK. TOMORROW'S WORLD.™

Brand message

Caterpillar has built a tight brand around values of rugged durability, reinforced by product design (a distinctive yellow color) and a responsive, proactive customer service.

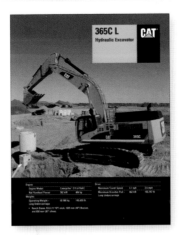

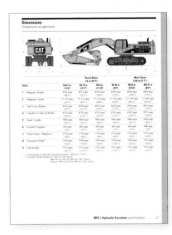

Services

Services are intrinsically different from products in one crucial way. While a product is always the same—consumer products strive for consistency—a service depends on human performance for its delivery, and is therefore subject to all the vagaries of humans' daily inconsistencies.

This is significant for branding, because while a product can be branded once and then benignly neglected for a while, a service requires the constant training (and motivation, support, and correction) of the people who deliver it to customers. This is as true for top corporate consultants as it is for staff at the local Burger King. Internal branding is critical to service industries. You must sell to your own people before you can sell to customers, because without employees who believe in the brand, it's impossible to get customers to believe.

Hospitality

The hospitality industry is enormous, including not only hotels, resorts, spas, and restaurants, but also, in a broader sense, every retail establishment on Main Street.

Every restaurant in the world should pride itself on its cuisine, but a great restaurant also cares about the quality of its service, the skill of its maître d', the stylishness of its architecture and décor, and little things like fresh flowers on the table. Attention to these other factors is what turns a good restaurant into a great hospitality brand.

What distinguishes a popular downtown bar from a deadly dull one? If you list the things that make the good bar better, they'll mostly fall into the "hospitality" category: the friendliness of the bartenders, the coziness of the seating, the lighting, the music … and inevitably, the other patrons who are attracted by these factors. This is another example of how customers share the role of defining a brand.

When people are asked what business McDonald's is in, many say "hamburgers." Some will say "family entertainment." A few smart ones will even say "real estate," on the assumption that acquiring lots of prime business locations is where the fast-food chain makes its real money. Yet McDonald's, like every other restaurant, is in the business of providing hospitality. Plenty of restaurants make a better hamburger; plenty provide better hospitality. But none provide the two so cheaply, reliably, and ubiquitously. That's where McDonald's has built its historic brand strength.

Hotels also base their brands on hospitality, since there isn't much else to differentiate one clean bed from another. Retail stores distinguish themselves by the range of goods they stock, but the best ones also know that hospitality is what puts a store's brand on a higher level. (The best retail chains have managed to apply their brands to the very products they sell: clothing chains such as Gap, H&M, Benetton, Mexx, and Mango are essentially extending a hospitality brand to sweaters and socks.)

At the heart of any hospitality brand are a well-designed environment and well-trained staff. The environment is the relatively easy part; it only needs to be solved once. Staff training is a continuous challenge, even at the best-run chains. Once staff are trained, they need to be motivated to embody the brand promise every day. Some restaurants

are too cool to ask their staff to smile; but McDonald's promises free food to any customer who isn't greeted with a smile. (I've never actually tried to claim this reward, although I'm sure I've had opportunities.) Other ways in which staff become part of the hospitality brand include being well informed about the products they're selling, acting out the brand personality, being helpful when customers have a complaint, and passing customer feedback along to managers who can fix things.

A brand is not going to overcome basic problems like bad food, lumpy mattresses, unstylish goods, or careless staff, but it can distill the experience of enjoying good food, comfy furniture, attractive merchandise, and attentive staff into an essential idea, different from the competitors, and present that idea to customers in a desirable way.

Identity and printed materials
Designed by Inaria. Original Travel specializes in "the big short break"–long weekends to destinations that are usually associated with much longer vacations. Their typical customer is cash-rich, but time-poor, so it was vital that the brand identity and printed materials appeal to refined tastes. The strategy was to break free from the tired conventions of the typical travel brochure, and craft something like a luxurious coffee-table book. The elegant result, with a plain cover in a unique shade of steely blue, breathtaking photography, and meticulous attention paid to production details, won awards and set a new standard for the high-end travel industry.

BeeLine
Where the Russian name
for cell-phone company
BeeLine is a pun on the
Russian for honeycomb,
the company's logo visually
references a bee's stripes.

Билайн™

Orange print ads
Illustrations by Emily Alston.
Departing from its initial
campaigns, which featured
stark photography of friendly,
everyday objects, the visuals
for Orange, the UK cell-phone
brand, take on a charming,
whimsical dimension that
set the brand apart from
its competitors and draw
customers into a storyline.

Banking and insurance

Financial services brands must do one
thing better than any other brands—inspire
trust. This was once accomplished through
naming (First National City Bank sounds like
an institution worthy of trust) and through
architecture (imposing facades giving the
impression of strength and longevity).
Nowadays banks use subtler forms of image
building. In addition to trust, competence,
and permanence, a financial brand must
stand out in a crowded field, encourage
clients to diversify, and most of all, to break
off relationships with competing banks.

Geico, an American insurance firm, offered
a high level of efficiency and personal phone
service at a cost well below other firms.
They realized they could do better with
a stronger brand image. Using humorous
ad campaigns, including one with a talking
gecko, Geico began pushing the catchy
claim that "15 minutes could save you

15 percent" and "we just want to save you money." But the brand goes beyond humorous advertising. A human, not an automated system, answers the phone, and the service is efficient. Plenty of brands have funny ads; Geico's not only provide humor, they also make a relevant point about the brand benefits.

The ads of one competitor protest "No cute talking lizards, just lower rates," but the competitor's weak branding only serves to keep Geico uppermost in customers' minds. The competition may offer lower rates, but the brand is uninspiring.

Telecommunications

Telecommunications firms face the considerable challenge of making complex technology accessible and attractive to ordinary customers. Almost all telecom firms have similar offerings: their brands have to be built on ease of use and superior customer service.

The first breakthrough brand in telecoms was Orange, created by Wolff Olins in the mid-1990s. From the start, Orange was about simplicity and friendliness. Its advertising, website, and brochures sported a minimalist look, with slender, orange type offsetting abstract, black-and-white photographs of everyday objects. The logo was a simple square. The design has since evolved and adapted, but the friendly, "different" ethos of the brand remains.

The first Orange shops, opened in the late 1990s, were designed according to the principles of feng shui—the firm originated in Hong Kong—and included tanks of goldfish for good luck. More recent shops are marked simply "Not Another Phone Shop." Inside, the walls are papered with pictures users have taken with their phones. Customers are offered coffee and free phone cleanings or support to encourage them to visit regularly.

Wolff Olins is also responsible for the identity of BeeLine, a leading Russian cell-phone brand. The name BeeLine is a play on words: a beeline being the shortest distance between two people, and "line" picking up on the Russian word for mobile phone, the first part of which also means "honeycomb." The absence of naming clichés like "-tel," "-cell," "-com," or "-net" set BeeLine apart from its competition.

BeeLine's original look was created in 1993. The logo launched in 2005—an elegant, abstract combination of a bee and a globe—is clean and stylish. Compared with the old version, the new identity is sophisticated and worldly, and reflects service rather than technology. The redesign showed that the brand was responsive to customers' changing expectations, and fitted the image they desired.

Many countries' local mobile/cellular/wireless brands have been taken over by global giants such as Vodafone, Orange, and T-Mobile. Unfortunately, the multinationals have focused more on financial gain than on brand insights, so each has struggled to build a meaningful worldwide identity that is persuasive to customers in the local markets. Not everyone wants to be part of a global colossus; some customers prefer their own, local identity and are no longer certain what to expect from their switched-over telecom brands.

Airlines and transportation

Airlines, cruise lines, train companies, and bus lines are in the business of getting people from one place to another. They can also be regarded as hospitality services.

Once upon a time, most airlines were national enterprises, flying the flag in a heavily regulated industry. This has begun to change, slowly, as low-cost carriers pressure the inefficient state-run companies to become more responsive to customers.

SAS is one of the best examples of an airline that successfully ditched its old way of thinking and developed a compelling new brand. The environments, both on board and in airport lounges, epitomize Scandinavian modernity. Luggage tags are inscribed with poetry rather than just a logo. The brand has become an identifiable mind-set for the whole organization.

One of the ways in which the airline industry has responded to its difficulties has been to form groupings between carriers, the major ones being Star Alliance, OneWorld, and SkyTeam. But while these partnerships may have some financial payoffs, the brand implications are more awkward. Although the attraction of national carriers persists— British Airways felt a serious backlash when it tried to reposition itself as a more worldly brand—a brand strategy that focuses more on customer experience than on cost-cutting would certainly be an improvement over the present situation.

Airline groupings
At one point Star Alliance went so far as to plaster some of its aircraft with the logos of all 12 members together! What this says to customers is that the individual brands are interchangeable and, therefore, meaningless. It would make more sense for each grouping to develop a single brand to replace the national carriers.

THE SUNDAY TIMES

The Moscow Times
SINCE 1992

Shared names
The New York Times has a strong name and a widely recognized logo. What role does the place name play in the brand? Could its name be shortened without any consequent loss of the newspaper's value? Most of the other *Times* newspapers around the world are unrelated companies. How will the similarities of names and logos be resolved in the future?

Media

The media, from giants like News Corporation and TimeWarner to bloggers and YouTube, began in seventeenth-century London coffeehouses. The telegraph, high-speed presses, radio, TV, and the Internet have all brought change, but the business model is the same: selling readers gossip, news, and critiques; and charging businesses to advertise. Journalistic standards are but one way of safeguarding a brand.

Old media brands are being challenged by specialized satellite and cable channels; magazines printed for niche audiences; and websites based on user content, such as Wikipedia and YouTube. Any bright child can set up a blog or podcast and reach much the same audience that Rupert Murdoch can. What are the prospects for big-media brands, hit by journalistic scandal, relegated behind the brands of their stars, their markets cannibalized? A brand should exploit every element to fulfill its goals (audience, point of view, content, revenue).

The name usually draws on a place name (*Sydney Morning Herald*), a founder's name (Forbes), a name that conveys corporate power (Columbia Broadcasting System), or the special interest served (The Food Network). *The Guardian* began its life based in Manchester, England, but dropped the city name from its title in a successful effort to reach audiences farther afield. *The New York Times* has no such need: its full name has a strong association with quality journalism, and its association with New York, center of finance and media, doesn't hurt. One future challenge will be what to do about the many other papers named "... *Times*," as geographic separation of markets disappears and media become more global.

The context of the logo must also be considered. A logo in the corner of a TV screen must be legible but not distracting. A distinctive outline works better than a bold, simple shape. MTV was the first channel to use hyperactive logo animation in the US, and this has now been widely adopted.

Broadcast presenters
Walter Cronkite was called "the most respected man in America." His power over public opinion was greater than that of President Johnson, who decided not to run for reelection partly as a result of Cronkite's bleak assessment of the Vietnam War. When Cronkite retired from CBS, the channel's brand went into decline. In retrospect, Walter Cronkite's personal brand was much stronger than that of CBS, whose evening news never regained its former popularity after he retired.

CBS◉

CBS logo
CBS's simple logo, designed by William Golden in 1951, conveys two ideas in one: the camera's lens and the viewer's eye. Unfortunately, the brand image has been diluted through inconsistent use of typography and incorporation of the "eye" into the logotypes of various related companies.

Newspaper banner logos must remain distinct at a distance. The typeface has to reflect the values of the paper; be emblematic of the place in which it is published (if it is a local paper), or transcend national characteristics (if it aspires to be a global paper); be legible in tiny web banners; and above all, have a timeless quality. Readers will have to look at it every day for decades without growing sick of it.

Magazines face even greater visual competition for both nameplate and cover art. Each cover needs to grab attention with an enticing visual image, and to evoke recognition with a distinctive, familiar nameplate and typographic style. It needs to combine the timely elements of the magazine's current coverage with the longer-term values that its readers expect. And it needs to be designed and printed quickly.

Broadcast media rely on presenters (anchors) to give them an appealing face. The best anchors achieve wide recognition and become brands in their own right. Walter Cronkite, often referred to as "the most respected man in America," retired as anchor of "CBS Evening News" in 1981, and the show's popularity declined. So which brand was driving the program's success: CBS's or Cronkite's?

Sports "tribes"
Sports teams offer fans an endless assortment of paraphernalia—from clothing to dolls to wall art—by which they can show off their loyalty and immerse themselves in the brand experience. Displaying one's sports affiliation promotes an intense bonding experience that can only be approximated by brands in other areas.

Sports

Some of the fiercest forms of brand loyalty pertain to sports. Whatever the psychological reasons, identification with a team and with one's fellow fans can be so intense that metaphors like "nation" and "tribe" are routinely used to describe sports fans. In larger cities which boast several teams for a given sport, the rivalries can be intense. Some interestingly subtle factors separate one set of fans from the other, such as class, education, income, and family background.

For example, New York's two baseball teams, the Yankees and the Mets, appeal to different groups of fans according to class, local geography, and personality. The parameters of these groups do overlap, but generally speaking, the Yankees appeal to working- and upper-class New Yorkers; the Mets appeal to the middle class. The Yankees draw fans with aspirations for success and little tolerance for mediocrity; the Mets, whose players seem to rotate more often, have toiled stoically at the

middle or bottom of their league for most of the team's history. Yankees fans value the club's long history, which includes legendary players Babe Ruth and Joe DiMaggio, and a record number of championships. The Mets, established in 1962, have won the championship only twice. Their slogan is "Ya gotta believe." Yankees fans generally tolerate the Mets as one would a pesky younger sibling; many Mets fans despise the Yankees.

Brand image reinforces both teams' loyalties. The team colors, the hospitality they show to fans, public pronouncements of the team's players and management, and players' behavior all reinforce the team brand. Several observers have noted that the appeal teams hold for their fans can be instructive about the appeal of brands in general as "tribal" identifiers.

Organizations

Developing and applying an integrated, sensible brand for a large organization is a daunting, long-term task, with uncertain results. Multinational corporations such as BP have completely redefined their brands, as have some notable nonbusiness organizations, including not-for-profit and educational organizations, although these have generally taken longer than the corporate sector acknowledge the importance of developing coherent brand identities.

Monolithic corporations and conglomerates

Some mega-corporations have solved their branding issues by pretending they don't have a brand, choosing instead to focus on the brands of their individual business units, products, or services. Others, like Mitsubishi and GE, have opted instead for the long march of building and maintaining a corporate mega-brand. In the world of branding and marketing, opinions remain divided as to whether this is a good idea. The benefits seem to be primarily in business-to-business dealings, since consumers tend not to care as much about big, monolithic corporations as about things they can actually buy.

In the early 2000s BP, the multinational oil company formerly known as British Petroleum, decided to begin a process of transformation. Their first steps toward recasting the brand as "green energy" met with skepticism and outright derision. "Big Oil" is not known for its dedication to environmental sensitivity, and many doubted that BP was sincere. The new logo, a yellow-and-green sunburst, was mocked by some designers for its spare, geometric look.

BP appears to be succeeding in its attempts to lead the way in "clean" energy usage, supporting technologies that reduce carbon emissions and investing in solar power. Although it still has some serious issues to overcome, BP's actions show that its new brand is not a simple veneer, but a representation of real commitment.

Governments, nongovernment and nonprofit organizations

What's the difference between branding a nation and branding a government? The two intersect in a number of ways. After all, it is usually governments that sponsor programs of national or regional branding.

One difference is that nation branding tends to be aimed outwards, at visitors and investors, while governmental branding tends to be aimed inward, at its own citizens. In most countries there is little or no concerted effort at projecting a coherent identity beyond using official names and coats of arms. However, there are a few democracies, mostly European, in which more progressive governments have come to understand that a good branding program can give the illusion of a participatory democracy by making government services easier to navigate, more responsive to the people and, because of their greater success in satisfying the demands of the electorate, more effective in power.

Green BP

While one of BP's slogans is "Beyond Petroleum," the initials now serve as the company name, rather than an acronym for it.

WWF trademark

Whether a corporation, a nonprofit, or a state-owned entity, the same concerns affect brand identity: appealing to the customer, reflecting the organization's values, and expressing its mission. The WWF's panda connotes both urgency and the wisdom required for the stewardship of nature.

State railway brand

Danish State Railways (DSB) were reorganized in 1999—from a government department to a state-owned company—and given a new identity to match their new mission of becoming more businesslike and competing for customers across Europe. The DSB identity includes a logo that is modern, yet classic; a distinctive typeface; and a look that reflects the Danish design aesthetic, famous around the world.

In most cases a brand needs to reflect the long-term mandate of the civil services, and of social structures such as welfare or development initiatives. Other entities, such as political parties, the armed forces, utilities, and transport systems, have used branding systems of one sort or another for a longer time, though with mixed results.

Many government entities, even today, can do a lot more to brand themselves successfully. The experience of governments in countries such as Denmark and Austria has shown that appropriate branding results in a better functioning of some of the apparatus of a democratic society, such as public administrations and services, because the mission becomes clearer and government employees have a better understanding of their own roles, and of their customers.

Nongovernmental organizations, because they need to raise a broad awareness of their work and compete to raise funds, have had more long-standing experience with the process of branding themselves than State entities. Because they are motivated by causes rather than profit, they also tend to be "ahead of the curve" in focusing on issues such as environmental friendliness, ethics, animal rights, and sustainable development. This has an obvious impact on their operations, and also on their brands.

Universities, churches, and museums

In *Branded Nation*, Professor James Twitchell examines the branding of these three types of institutions in the US. That they need branding as much as anything should come as no surprise. Universities, whether public or private, have multiple customers: prospective and current students; faculty and staff; alumni, who may donate money; and the general public, whose opinion of the school affects issues such as government funding, esteem for the professors and their publications, and how popular the school's sports teams are.

A brand needs to address all of these groups. The school brand will be influenced by its location (or origin brand), the renown of its founders and leaders, the history and caliber of academic inquiry there, and (especially in the US) how well the football team does. Most schools measure academic performance factors obsessively, and the general public tends to follow the results with some interest. So in theory, marketers of university brands should have an easier job. But in practice the many stakeholders, and the general aloofness of academia concerning commercial things like brands, mean that anyone managing a university brand faces a big challenge.

It may seem odd, even heretical, to discuss the branding of religion, but in fact religious movements were some of the earliest adopters of signs and symbols, and religious leaders throughout the ages have had a good grasp of the correlation between a clear message and a loyal following.

Douglas Atkin, in *The Culting of Brands*, draws a persuasive (if slightly overstated) parallel between brand affinity and belonging to a religious group. The Bible contains a seminal lesson about idol worship that is instructive to brand managers: don't bow down before the logo, but pay attention to the transcendent meaning of the brand and live by its dictums.

Recently, so-called megachurches in the US have found that ordinary branding, positioning, and marketing strategies work. There is nothing intrinsically different about a religious congregation that negates the rules of branding as they apply to any other organization.

Museums have many of the same issues, goals, and stakeholder groups as universities (minus the football teams, of course). They need to appeal not only to their regular patrons and supporters, but also to the general public, and to maintain esteem and funding in order to ensure that they continue to have the means of carrying out their stated mission of enlightenment. Some museums brand themselves as part of an establishment; others court controversy and try to keep their brand edgy. A clever few are able to appear edgy while reassuring the establishment.

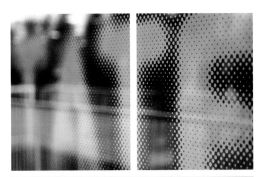

Gallery brands

This long-standing London gallery began expanding to new locations in the 1980s and needed to redefine its brand. With help from Wolff Olins, Tate reinvented the idea of a gallery from a single, institutional museum, with a single, institutional view, to a branded collection of experiences: sharing an attitude, but offering many different ways of seeing.

Places

Every place is a brand—nations, regions, cities, districts, streets, even individual shopping malls and individual buildings. Whether as an origin or a destination, a place to buy things from, or a place to travel to or invest in, most people want their "home" to be perceived positively. Places compete to find markets for their exports and to attract tourism and investment money.

Many residents are aware that the way outsiders perceive them could do with a little improvement. The bigger the place, the more people have a stake in building its brand, and the longer it takes. A building can be branded in a matter of weeks; a country may take a generation or more to alter its brand image.

Nations and regions

The birthplace—or origin brand—is a fundamental component of many exports. Nationality is a key attribute of German cars and Swiss chocolate, English clothes and American sportswear, French wine and Japanese electronics. Many people believe Italian olive oil is the best in the world; while many other Mediterranean nations produce olive oil of equal or better quality, the Italians have done a superior job of developing their olive-oil-origin brand.

Many local brands take their nationality with them when they go global and use it to differentiate themselves from their international competition. For example, many countries brew good pilsner, but the Czechs have managed to exploit their status as "the birthplace of Pilsner" to make their brand successful.

What is the difference between clothing "made in China" and clothing "made in Italy" to people around the world today? What do the Chinese hope their origin brand will mean 20 years from now? One of the issues that countries like China, India, Russia, and Brazil need to deal with as they establish their local brands in a global market, is how to turn their nation-brands from being a hindrance to being a help.

Taiwan went through this in the 1990s. The slogan "It's very well made in Taiwan" was a clear attempt to deal with the fact that many people around the world viewed the "made in Taiwan" label as an indication of low price and quality, even though the quality was often fine. In Taiwan's case, the problem was mostly with foreign perception, so an advertising campaign was an appropriate solution.

Ironically, developing nations often seem more aware of the need to develop their destination brand than their Western counterparts. Brand development needs to be well coordinated among authorities at all levels. It is sometimes more of a challenge to get this focus in a developed, liberal democracy than in other societies which have more at stake. Some of the best examples of destination brands come from small, developing countries, such as Guatemala and Estonia.

Guatemala *alma de la tierra*

Destination brands
Identity by Interbrand. Most destination brands aim to improve perceptions in order to increase tourism or investment, as does this campaign for Guatemala. Some simply aim to improve quality of life by boosting civic pride. In either case, the success of the branding program rests on broad acceptance of and adherence to the branding guidelines by the many, many parties that have a stake in the place: residents, businesses, public organizations, government offices, and state-run entities such as transport networks.

Branding a locality
Even as small an area as a few blocks within a city can be branded, as this identity by Pentagram for New York's Fashion Center Business Improvement District demonstrates. The clever icon was transformed into an arresting piece of public sculpture propped on an information booth. This welcomes visitors to the neighborhood that was traditionally called the Garment District.

Buildings and developments

Sometimes it seems as though every architect and real-estate developer wants their building to be a brand. This is easily achieved if the location is already a prime one, if the architect is a well-known brand in his or her own right, or if the developer has an established market presence. In other cases, it is necessary to start from scratch. A building can benefit from a strong micro-destination brand in obvious ways: more visitors, higher rent, a higher rate of occupancy. But a good building brand also benefits the brand of the city or region the building is in, and vice versa, and naturally the tenants' own brands gain by association.

Bluewater
KENT

The elements of a building's brand can include a prestigious address, good architecture, an attractive identity (mostly expressed through signage and advertising), and the right mix of support services for tenants and visitors. In some cases, the association with the developer or architect also has lasting value for the brand.

Bluewater shopping mall
Design by Minale Tattersfield Design Strategy. The visual identity for this retail and entertainment complex in the south of England draws on traditional symbols of the surrounding area: blue lakes and the white horse of Kent. The identity, introduced in 1999, is applied primarily to signage. Its success has drawn visitors from as far afield as France and Belgium.

Portfolios and case studies

There are as many creators of brands and brand identities in the world as there are entrepreneurs and designers. What follows is the work of a dozen firms that do this excellently. In fact, they have created identities for some of the world's most recognized and effective brands. Still, this is a very small sampling of the world's branding practitioners, and there are many others I would have liked to include here that I could not, due simply to limitations of space and time.

Some of the outfits here began life as part of an advertising agency. Others grew out of graphic design studios. Some set out to identify themselves as practitioners of branding, while others have resisted that label and prefer to think of themselves as designers who happen to work on brands. Some of the firms here are global; others have remained local. All exhibit a passion for brands that makes their work exceptional.

I have presented some examples separately from the rest of the portfolios because I felt they were useful studies in how branding could resolve a particular issue or problem. I hope they succeed in illustrating some of the issues and questions addressed in the previous sections.

It will be apparent, looking through these portfolios, that no two firms approach the issues of branding in quite the same way, or reach the same solution. Each firm has its own strategy, its own creative direction, and its own way of implementing a brand identity. In effect, each firm has its own brand, reflected in the kinds of clients it attracts and the kinds of brand solutions it creates. By now, that should make perfect sense.

Regarded as a pioneer in the development of branding and visual identity as a strategic business tool, Landor was the first truly international branding and design firm. Established in 1941, it eventually opened offices in Asia, Europe, Latin America, and throughout the United States. Today, Landor Associates works with hundreds of clients on six continents, combining the resources of a global company with the access and familiarity of a local partner to provide a world of branding expertise.

A creative visionary, Walter Landor helped develop some of the world's most recognized brands and corporate identities, including Coca-Cola, Levi's, Kellogg's, GE, Fujifilm, Alitalia, 20th Century Fox, Singapore Airlines, 3M, the World Wildlife Fund, and Bank of America, among many others. He was a founding partner, with Misha Black and Milner Gray, in England's first industrial design consultancy, Industrial Design Partnership (IDP).

In 1939, Walter traveled to the United States as part of the design team for the British Pavilion at the New York World's Fair, and later settled in San Francisco. In 1941, he established Walter Landor & Associates in his small Russian Hill flat, with his wife Josephine as his first "associate." As his company grew, Landor became one of the first to use consumer research in packaging design, and is widely credited with establishing the economic value of design and effective visual communications in business. According to John Fleckner

communications, and the use of symbols and visual imagery is an essential part of the broader story of American culture and society in the last half century."

In 1964, Landor moved his firm to the ferryboat *Klamath*, anchored at San Francisco's Pier 5. The move to the *Klamath* greatly enhanced the company's reputation for innovation and creativity, and it also provided more space to expand the firm's design and consulting capabilities. Although Landor Associates eventually outgrew the ferryboat in the late 1980s, the *Klamath* remains the firm's symbol.

Acquired by Young & Rubicam in 1989, Landor Associates is now part of WPP Group. Walter Landor died in 1995.

Brocade

Brocade Communications Systems is the world leader in storage area networks (SANs), with Cisco Systems a primary competitor. After acquiring McDATA, another competitor, Brocade doubled its size, helping assure its leadership in SAN technology against Cisco. But even with record earnings and a plan for growth and diversification, Brocade recognized that its brand and business strategies needed to align in order to support future expansion. The company wanted to make sure the brand could maintain its leadership position with SAN's engineers while also reaching out to chief information officers (CIOs).

Through market shifts, acquisition, new management, and technology, Brocade had changed dramatically. Landor's research confirmed that Brocade understood the minds of its customers, and that customers were loyal. Nevertheless, Landor concluded that in its current state, Brocade stood little chance with the CIO audience, even though some aspects of the brand equity did appeal to the interests of CIOs. The challenge was to reposition Brocade around those parts of the equity, to become more relevant to the future CIO customer without alienating existing customers. The repositioning also needed to differentiate Brocade from a much larger, competitive set.

Using insights gained from research, Landor developed a "brand driver" dubbed Challenge with Intent, which evokes courage, being smart, motivation to do and be more, and staying "lean and mean" with focus and purpose. Landor designed the new identity system to better embody the insight of the brand and to signify Brocade's repositioning to the market visually.

BROCADE

Biltmore

The Biltmore Estate in Asheville, North Carolina, is the largest privately owned home in America. Built by George and Edith Vanderbilt in 1895, the Biltmore brand has grown considerably. Beyond the home and garden tour, the estate now includes America's most visited winery, a four-star inn, fabulous restaurants, and countless activities. Importantly, the Biltmore brand has also extended beyond the destination, selling wine at retail nationally, and offering Biltmore For Your Home interior products through retailers such as Lowe's and Belk.

Having acquired multiple identities and styles, the Biltmore Estate suffered a loss of strategic focus. Management realized they needed to define what the Biltmore brand stood for, and bring clarity to its brand equity and positioning. The new positioning and design system helps define Biltmore less as a destination and more as a lifestyle brand, and provides a platform for expansion.

Landor's positioning establishes the brand's originality, endorses "off the estate" ventures as authentically Biltmore, and highlights the consumer benefit of lifestyle inspiration. The design system, Spirit of Biltmore, brings the essence of the original Biltmore to life and offers a flexible graphic system for the brand's many ventures.

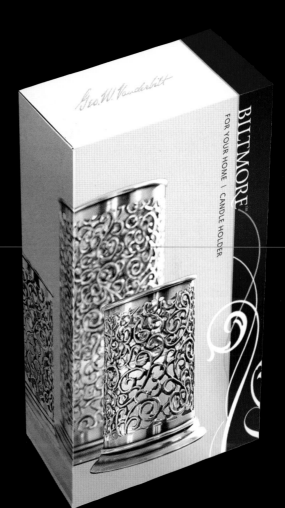

Sensata

In January 2006, Texas Instruments spun off its Sensors & Controls Division as an independent company that was a global leader in sensing and protection solutions. This company intended to invest in new technologies, break into new markets, and develop the talents of its employees. Landor was responsible for coming up with a new name, brand platform, visual identity, brandline, and brand voice.

The client had a 90-year heritage (longer than its parent Texas Instruments) and a market share of over 90% in key areas. Landor had the opportunity to build on that heritage and prestige while defining what the new brand would mean to customers and employees worldwide.

Landor developed the name Sensata Technologies to evoke an image of the company's business. Sensata is Latin for "those things gifted with sense," and also a modern word with positive meanings in Italian, Spanish, and Portuguese ("sensible, considered"). The visual identity was inspired by braille, the universal alphabet based on the sense of touch, and the various points and colors represent Sensata's diverse expertise, customer partnership, global reach, and employee base. The pattern of circles reflects the dynamic company culture—people finding new solutions using Sensata's solid portfolio of technology. The identity can also serve as a graphic element in printed and web communications.

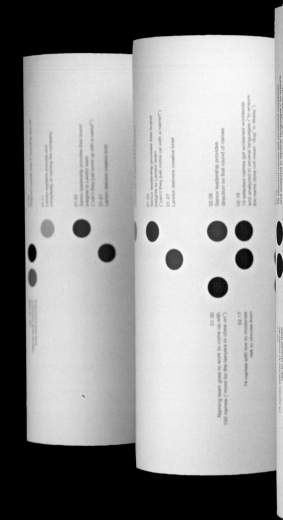

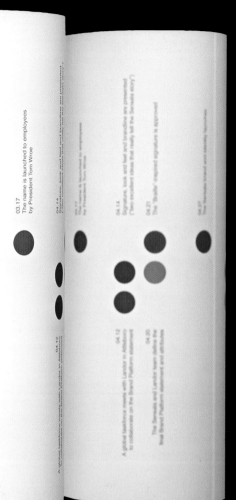

Sensata

Technologies

Tom Wroe   529 Pleasant Street, Attleboro, MA 02703
President   508 236-3333 Tel 508 236-2222 Fax
                     twroe@sensata.com

Nescafé

Nestlé's Nescafé is the leading instant-coffee brand in Australia. Nestlé decided to launch several new premium Nescafé products while refreshing the look of one of its best sellers, Nescafé Gold. One of the products introduced was the instant espresso-style coffee, Nescafé Short Black, for which Nestlé asked Landor to come up with conceptual branding and package design. As the first instant espresso product on the market, this was a unique brand and "proposition" within the highly competitive coffee category. The design needed to express cutting-edge sophistication.

Landor developed a simple, confident, elegant, and sensual package design. The design features the iconic image of *crema*, the delicious foam that appears on the top of an espresso. A halo-like rim evokes the product's perfection. The short jar shape (developed by D3 Design) reinforces the product's proposition. The sleek black color theme, understated typography, and minimal imagery all link back to what the product is about—a personal espresso experience combined with the convenience of instant preparation.

Fitch

Fitch's background in traditional retail design has expanded to encompass environments, product design, identity, communication, and strategy, including research into customer behavior and areas such as color and fashion.

Started by Rodney Fitch in 1972, the firm was listed on the stock exchange in 1982—the first design firm in the world to be recognized in this way. In 2001, Fitch became part of the WPP Group of advertising and marketing communications agencies; it now employs 500 people, in 18 studios, across 10 countries.

Fitch's clients include many of the best-known brands in the world, along with smaller companies. Together they cover nearly every market sector: automotive, retail, consumer goods and services, health care, fashion, financial and professional

Planet Hollywood Resort and Casino

As part of a top-to-bottom, retro-chic renovation, the Planet Hollywood Resort & Casino in Las Vegas asked Fitch to design three new stores named The Store, Stuff, and This & That.

The interior designs for The Store and Stuff are based on the elegance of "Old Hollywood," with art-deco styling, silver-leaf ceilings, and glossy finishes. These stores share a design language, yet maintain a distinct character. A strong visual presence is established through the deliberately conspicuous lighting scheme, in keeping with the spirit of Las Vegas.

The Store sells the latest Planet Hollywood sundries in the hotel lobby. It offers guests a rich environment in which to buy a piece of the Planet Hollywood Resort & Casino brand that they can take away. Stuff, with a design language that gives a modern twist to its merchandise, is visually distinct from the other stores. It is intended as a place where visitors can get all their favorite Planet Hollywood products. This & That is a highly designed one-stop-shop for snacks, drinks, magazines, and more, on the casino floor.

The three concept stores are intended to provide everything a visitor might desire, from T-shirts to suntan lotion.

e name LEGO comes from the Danish
g godt" which means "play well." (By
incidence, it also means "I connect"
"I put together" in Latin.) The "play well"
ilosophy has stayed with LEGO from its
tablishment in the 1930s, as a maker of
ooden toys—it has always focused on
aking the best-possible toys from the best-
ossible materials. Its innovations are well
own: from its pioneering use of injection-
olded plastics to its sponsoring of
ademic research into child's play.

When Fitch worked with LEGO to
evelop the concept for a new generation
branded stores, the aim was to create
entertaining and educational experience
ased on the concept of play: LEGO's brand
alues are creativity, imagination, and fun
a way that encourages learning. It was
so important that the retail environments
phold the quality and integrity of the brand.

of all ages, the store experience needed
to be stimulating and engaging for all.

Fitch designed the environment from the
child's perspective. This featured a central
"living room," comprised entirely of elements
colored in LEGO's particular shade of yellow,
where play and interaction are encouraged.
Product displays are planned according to
the average height of particular ages, the
color theme and arrangement give it a
friendly dimension, and design touches
like the pick-a-brick containers, arranged
to resemble the studs on a Lego piece,
reinforce the satisfaction of the toy itself.

The award-winning design has been
rolled out at a number of locations across
the UK, Europe, and the USA. Both sales
performance and customer response have
been positive, demonstrating that a well-
designed environment can contribute to
the strength of the LEGO brand overall.

Mint Museum

Singapore is home to one of the world's largest private toy collections. Its owner asked Fitch to create the name and branding for a museum to house it. Mint Museum of Toys, the world's first purpose-built toy museum, opened in Singapore in May 2006. It showcases a world-class collection of mint-condition toys from the nineteenth and twentieth centuries, and includes a café and shop. The museum is aimed primarily at adults wanting to indulge their childhood nostalgia. Its ambition is to encourage visitors to rediscover the things "that help us imagine and play."

Fitch's solution echoes this ambition through a visual language that is sophisticated, witty, and playful. Carefully selected toys from the collection are used to communicate specific messages. On the café menu, Popeye encourages visitors to eat their greens; a 1960s toy rocket propels the museum lifts; and the ropes on Betty Boop's swing become the handles of the branded carrier bags. Every message is visual, playful, and inventive. No two pieces of communication look the same, and each puts the individuality of the toys at its heart. The deft mix of subject matter, typography, and color create an identity that captures the nostalgia and fun of vintage toys, yet

Hanson Dodge Creative

From its beginnings in a spare bedroom, with just a handful of clients, Ken Hanson's graphic design firm developed on the basis of his drive to produce design that achieved results. As the business grew, he became partners with Tim Dodge, who was providing business representation to graphic artists.

Today, Hanson Dodge Creative is one of the leading American brand experience experts serving the active lifestyle marketplace. The drive and ambition that characterizes its work has led to a portfolio that is heavy on clients from the world of sports, exercise, and outdoor activity.

Hanson Dodge's offering runs the gamut from strategy to execution, with an uncommon focus on precision in and effectiveness of the creative solution. In this sense, the firm itself is well branded: they are what they do. And they are equally comfortable working with niche clients and with those whose market is more general.

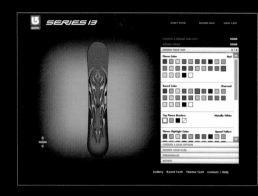

Burton Snowboards

Working in partnership with Burton Snowboards, Hanson Dodge launched the Series 13 custom board program—the first of its kind in the industry. The program seamlessly integrated Burton's internal manufacturing, distribution, and independent-dealer network with an online experience for customers. The Series 13, which enabled riders to design their own boards, launched to rave reviews and helped continue Burton's leading position.

Trek bicycles

Back in 1976, Trek consisted of five employees making bikes out of a barn in Waterloo, Wisconsin, USA. Thirteen years later, the company had grown exponentially, and Trek partnered with Hanson Dodge to take the next step of shifting from a product focus to customers' real-world experiences. More than just design, the new brand focus influenced just about every part of Trek's business, from sales promotion to long-term strategic planning. Since the partnership began, Hanson Dodge has helped Trek grow its sales nearly tenfold.

Johnson Outdoors

Between them, Old Town Canoe Co., Necky Kayaks, and Ocean Kayak offer canoes and kayaks for everyone, from traditionalists to hard-core enthusiasts, and casual paddlers. However, these three Johnson Outdoors brands were not communicating their distinctive characteristics: Old Town's 100-year heritage, Ocean's laid-back appeal, or Necky's high-tech innovation. Hanson Dodge's strategy captured each brand's personality, and conveyed it in user-friendly websites and new print advertising.

Wolverine Boots and Shoes

In 2006, Hanson Dodge partnered with Wolverine Boots and Shoes on a complete redesign of their website. The primary goal was to create a dynamic web experience that would ultimately allow the brand to expand from a shoes-only offering to a global, head-to-toe lifestyle brand. The Hanson Dodge creative strategy shifted the brand's visual representation away from an "epic" approach to one that featured new visuals, unique to the Wolverine brand. This imagery succeeded in bringing a more personal nature to the site, while remaining true to the brand's "relentless by nature" positioning. This effort was supported by a launch promotion, entitled "I am Wolverine," in which users were encouraged to submit personal stories and photographs of their experiences with Wolverine products.

Inaria

Inaria is a twenty-first-century design and branding firm. Founded in 2000 by Andrew Thomas and Debora Berardi, and based in London, Inaria has chosen to focus on design with a sophisticated, innovative look. This is well suited to luxury brands, be they in fashion, hospitality, or travel, and also succeeds in adding value to clients in areas such as information technology and charity.

Much of the agency's work consists of printed editorial pieces, such as brochures, reports, and corporate communications. All is designed with a beautifully crafted elegance that immediately conveys the passion, commitment, and vision of the brands in question.

Of course, being a twenty-first-century agency means digital media are key to Inaria's capabilities: much of their work is also for the web, where the sophisticated look of their print projects translates remarkably well, defying expectations and achieving a cross-platform consistency that is uncommonly crisp, even in the age of Web 2.0.

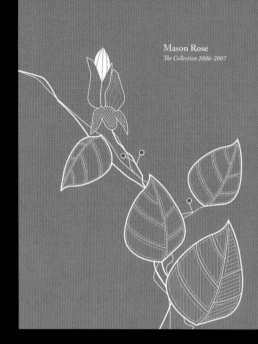

Mason Rose
The Collection 2006-2007

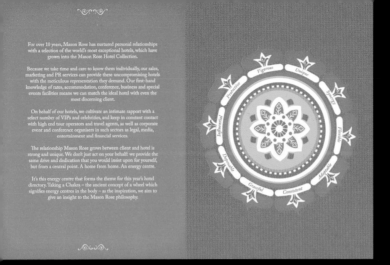

For over 10 years, Mason Rose has nurtured personal relationships with a selection of the world's most exceptional hotels, which have grown into the Mason Rose Hotel Collection.

Because we take time and care to know them individually, our sales, marketing and PR services can provide these uncompromising hotels with the meticulous representation they demand. Our first-hand knowledge of rates, accommodation, conference, business and special events facilities means we can match the ideal hotel with even the most discerning client.

On behalf of our hotels, we cultivate an intimate rapport with a select number of VIPs and celebrities, and keep in constant contact with high end tour operators and travel agents, as well as corporate event and conference organisers in such sectors as legal, media, entertainment and financial services.

The relationship Mason Rose grows between client and hotel is strong and unique. We don't just act on your behalf: we provide the same drive and dedication that you would insist upon for yourself, but from a central point. A home from home. An energy centre.

It's this energy centre that forms the theme for this year's hotel directory. Taking a Chakra – the ancient concept of a wheel which signifies energy centres in the body – as the inspiration, we aim to give an insight to the Mason Rose philosophy.

Mason Rose hotel directory

For over 10 years, Mason Rose has represented luxury hotels around the world. Its product knowledge, attention to detail, and exceptional service are second to none. It produces an annual directory detailing each hotel, and with each entry occupying four pages, it is vital that the personality of Mason Rose is not overpowered by the hotels themselves. To ensure this wasn't the case, divider pages were introduced to add personality and visual pace.

Inaria recognized that the value of the divider pages could be increased if they were as business-focused as they were creative. Their solution was to draw parallels between a chakra—the ancient concept of a wheel that signifies energy centers in the body— and the energy center that Mason Rose provides for its clients. The core business and service attributes were then brought to life through rose illustrations, and a further parallel drawn between the characteristics of the rose and the brand itself.

One&Only

One&Only is a selection of the world's most beautiful and original resorts. Although there are seven, each is unique. To capture this visually, each resort has its own brand identity, the inspiration for which comes from the local culture, environment, flora, or fauna. These seven identities are unified through the One&Only logotype; a distinctive typeface selection; a consistent photographic style, tone of voice, and format; and an overriding sense of quality, fun, and luxury.

As One&Only Reethi Rah, Maldives was the first resort in One&Only's portfolio to be built from scratch, it was also the first time the client needed every collateral item to be created simultaneously. This offered an unprecedented opportunity for design and production consistency, but the fact that over 160 projects needed to be delivered to the Maldives during a six-month period meant that the logistics were as crucial to the success of the project as the creative and production input. The work included all back-office stationery; in-villa items; the boutique packaging, bags, and gift boxes; the spa collateral; lavish restaurant menus and waterproof poolside menus; and marketing items such as CD sleeves, e-marketing campaigns, brochures, and invitations. Ensuring that the minutest details were considered—matching the hot-pink tissue paper from China exactly to the hot-pink ribbon from Japan—was key to producing collateral material that consistently met the brand standards.

Throughout their work with One&Only, Inaria have been able to use their in-depth knowledge of print production to produce luxurious brochures and directories, often with special effects such as hard covers and debossed graphics, at considerable savings. The One&Only newsletter maintains the brand's high standards, striking a balance between dense content and opulent white space. The choice of bulky paper with more air in it improves the tactile quality, and also offers a saving on postage costs.

Invitations to launch the resort at Reethi Rah were foil blocked in metallic copper onto a 7mm (c. 4in) thick, dark brown board, packaged with a brochure in a bespoke box and tied with silk ribbon. The guest's name was added by a calligraphy expert, and the package was hand-delivered with an orchid, the symbol of the resort.

To meet the need for beautiful, tactile menu covers that were also durable, mark-resistant, and easy to update, case-bound covers were wrapped with semi-coarse fabric and foil-blocked with metallic copper. Inserts are held through a variety of innovative binding techniques which allow the resort to add updates easily and cost-effectively.

Mauritius

One&Only Le Touessrok

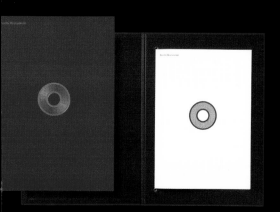

One&Only Le Touessrok
Playground of love and life

Xtreme Information

Xtreme Information collects advertising. With an archive of over 6 million ads, it holds one of the world's largest collections of print and screen advertising, which is growing at a rate of 60,000 new ads per month. The most interesting aspect of Xtreme's business is the competitive intelligence that can be gained from all this information. For example, advertisers can find out exactly how, where, and when their competitors are advertising; how much they are spending; and their marketing trends, core themes, and media plans. Advertising agencies can view the latest creative work, discover new marketing techniques, or gain invaluable insight into potential clients' ad spend, ensuring that their creative ideas are linked to a realistic budget.

All this information is sold through 13 separately branded products, many offering progressive amounts of the same information, and many being relevant to more than one of Xtreme's four key target markets. This complexity makes Xtreme's offer difficult to explain to potential customers, and challenging to understand. Xtreme therefore required a brochure that would act as an introduction to its overall offer, and as a product directory. It had to be easily understood by "cold" prospects, but was also required as a selling aid in face-to-face meetings.

Although the product structure is complex, its story is essentially straightforward: Xtreme offers the knowledge clients need in order to gain a competitive advantage in their marketplace. This idea formed the main structure of the book and was told through a simple concept: Vision + Knowledge = Intelligence. The book is divided into three sections with the first, Vision, giving an overview of Xtreme's proposition while asking the reader to imagine the results if they had this information at their fingertips. Working alongside illustrator Paul Davis, Inaria created illustrations throughout this section to represent the quick doodles of someone sketching out ideas on a piece of paper. The second section, Knowledge, details all the products within the portfolio. Illustrated with screen grabs, charts, graphs, and magazine spreads, this section features one product per spread and gives an instant insight into the benefits of each brand. The third and final section, Intelligence, explains how each client type can gain the competitive intelligence and advantage needed in an everchanging marketplace through combining the products that Xtreme offers.

VISION + KNOWLEDGE = INTELLIGENCE

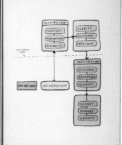

IMAGINE THE RESULTS

COMPETITIVE ADVANTAGE

INTELLIGENCE

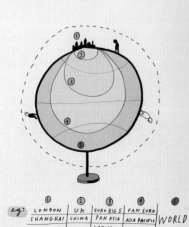

IMAGINE INTERNATIONAL ADVERTISING AT YOUR FINGERTIPS, AS GLOBAL OR AS LOCAL AS YOU NEED IT

Anti-Slavery International

Anti-Slavery International is the world's oldest international human rights organization. It was founded in 1839 by a group of individuals who had worked with slavery abolitionists—including Buxton, Clarkson, and Wilberforce—in their fight to ban slavery and the slave trade within the British colonies. Today the organization exposes current cases of slavery, campaigns for those enslaved to be freed, and supports the initiatives of local organizations to release people through pressing for the more effective implementation of international laws against slavery.

Since 2002 Inaria have worked *pro bono* for Anti-Slavery International, the only charity in the UK working exclusively against slavery and related abuses. Its fund-raising ball is an essential part of the charity's income. Each ball, held at a top London hotel, is supported by some of the UK's leading organizations and is attended by over 500 guests.

Rather than resorting to hackneyed depictions of liberty, Inaria's design work emphasizes themes of human dignity and self-esteem. The result is a profoundly compelling communication that draws attention not only to the ongoing existence of slavery, but also to its very human costs. Every year a theme is chosen to ensure that while the seriousness of the message is delivered, the evening is also a celebration of the positive steps being taken. Themes have included Colours of the World, Calypso, Rajasthan, and the Jungle. These offer scope for creativity and originality unbound

by strict brand identity guidelines, but still inspired by the ideals of the charity's mission. Inaria's belief is that the better the ball's program—produced in cooperation with Fulmar Colour Printing and Osier Graphics, with the donated talents of photographers such as Ben Rice—the more likely it is to be taken home by the guests. This offers a greater incentive to potential advertisers, allowing Anti-Slavery's message to resonate after the event, as well as giving the ball's committee members a better marketing tool for the following year. A testament to this strategy is that very few programs are left at the end of the evening, and sponsorship has increased year on year.

Calypso can be traced back to the arrival of the first slaves in Trinidad, brought to work on the sugar plantations.

COLOURS OF THE WORLD

Saturday 12th November 2005

The Grosvenor House Hotel, Park Lane, London
(Please use the Johnson entrance on Park Lane)

Reception 7.00pm **Carriages** 2.00am
Dress Colours of the World, Black Tie or National Dress

Please bring this ticket with you.

Sponsors Bombay Brasserie, Coca-Cola Africa, Palmer Colour Printing, Jemla, Nordstrom Press
Paper supplied by Howard French and GF Smith

anti-slavery
today's fight for tomorrow's freedom

Registered Charity No 1049160
www.antislavery.org

Firezza

Firezza opened its doors in 2001, allowing its two owners to realize a long-held ambition—to offer restaurant-quality, traditional Neapolitan pizza through a high-quality delivery service. They have won acclaim from critics and discerning foodies alike through their use of fresh ingredients and organic produce wherever possible. During its first five years, Firezza opened branches in six locations across London, and made plans for more.

Although initially relevant, the start-up identity was not reflective of Firezza's growing reputation as London's leading pizza-delivery restaurant. It didn't clearly define the company's brand proposition, and also undermined the quality of the product and service being offered. Inaria worked with Firezza to research and analyze the marketplace, define the company's brand strategy, and create an essence that aligned its offer with the needs of its target audience. Based on the belief that Mediterranean food can form the basis of a healthy diet, the brand strategy, identity, and claim all communicate the idea that quality pizza is possible through the use of natural, healthy ingredients. The symbol was inspired by a combination of natural forms and early Italian architectural ornament. The square format derives from the fact that Firezza sells pizza in the true Neapolitan way—by the meter. The clean, contemporary logotype clearly differentiates the brand's offer from the average fast-food outlet. The

symbol also forms the basis of a unique pattern, used as a secondary graphic device on packaging and all marketing material. The Firezza.com website was designed to be simple, informative, and graphically appealing, and to provide an opportunity for customers to give feedback. Contemporary typography and a clean layout, combined with black-and-white imagery, ensure that key information is predominant throughout.

If a brand sets out to challenge widely held perceptions within a sector and genuinely believes that its product or service is different from that of any of its competitors, it is essential that the brand identity be a reflection of this attitude. Working with Firezza's existing packaging printer, Inaria ensured that Firezza's delivery boxes, bags, and cartons looked significantly more distinctive, contemporary, and upmarket than their existing items, without increasing the production unit cost.

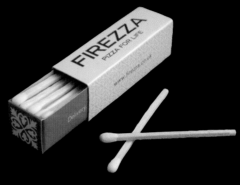

NetJets Europe

NetJets is the world's leading private aviation operator. Although the NetJets offer is predominantly service-orientated, its jets have such a high visual impact that photography plays a major role in the company's sales and marketing programs. Inaria was commissioned to art-direct a new photographic approach, covering two distinct areas. The first style was for "hero" shots of each plane within the fleet. Using lighting, multiple exposures, and expert retouching, photographer Tim Simmons transformed the picture of the plane he shot in a cramped corner of London City Airport on an overcast day into an iconic and awe-inspiring image.

The second photographic style aimed to capture the incredible attention to detail on each plane. From the designer-inspired interiors, such as the beautifully stitched leather seats, to the spotless engine cases themselves, photographer Ben Rice captured the refined elegance and immaculate design detailing that sets the NetJets aircraft apart.

As part of NetJets' rebranding project, Inaria was asked to create a website aimed specifically at the European market. The brief called for a site that was slick and sophisticated, with information easily accessible to the user. Flash animation allows flowing, effortless movement, and transitions evocative of the flawlessly streamlined service that NetJets provides. The wide-screen format allows NetJets' predominantly landscape images to be shown as effectively as possible, and the navigation completely "collapses," ensuring that the screen remains clutter-free. Within the site's Fleet section, the animated specifications and interactive range maps not only bring life to information, but also increase the user's understanding of the technical details presented.

Interbrand

Brands, according to Interbrand's website, "represent free choice. They also have a profound impact on our quality of life and the way we see our world. They color our lives. They reflect the values of our societies. Global brands act as ambassadors for nations and capture the spirit of an age."

Following the concept that a brand is essentially an idea, Interbrand is "dedicated to identifying, building, and expressing the right idea for a brand." And, of course, turning the expression of that idea into a solid business proposition for its clients, complete with financial benchmarks and measurable results. Interbrand is listed in *Guinness World Records* as the world's largest design firm. And speaking of Guinness, Interbrand put a value on that invaluable brand, too.

Besides brand valuation, Interbrand offers services that run the gamut from analysis and strategy to creativity and implementation, including the latest digital tools. Since opening its offices in London (1974) and New York (1979), Interbrand has grown to include more than 30 locations in 20 over countries. In the 1980s the organization made its mark in areas such as naming, coming up with now-familiar brand names like Prozac, HobNobs, and Slice.

In 1989, Interbrand pioneered valuation techniques by putting a price on the Pillsbury group of brands in preparation for their acquisition by Grand Met.

The 1990s saw the Interbrand network expand to become part of the Omnicom Group. Interbrand continued to create world-famous corporate identities (Imation, PricewaterhouseCoopers) and consumer brands (Deutsche Telekom, oneworld, Quilmes), and published a number of books on subjects such as trademark protection and co-branding.

In the new millennium the pace has continued, with dozens of new brands created or revitalized, and offices established in Shanghai, Moscow, and other cities around the world. Online, Interbrand produces brandchannel.com, which has become a force for spreading know-how and encouraging dialogue within the community of branding practitioners.

Of the many contributions Interbrand has made over the decades, perhaps the greatest has been to turn the field of branding into a serious discipline, demonstrating that brands can be managed as a large-scale enterprise, and that they deserve the attention of corporate boardrooms.

AT&T

AT&T is a large company with an illustrious history as a telecommunications firm, which it traces back to Alexander Graham Bell, inventor of the telephone. In the 1980s, judged too large and powerful, it was broken up into smaller, regional companies. Some of these, including SBC, were later reunited with AT&T through mergers. The result was a company that enjoyed widespread recognition in many areas of networking and telecommunications, but that had a fractured and inconsistent brand image which lacked coherence, and was in danger of being perceived as outmoded. However, this was balanced within the company by a good organizational understanding of who the customer was and what they wanted.

Interbrand tackled the strategy by first surveying different parts of AT&T's market to find out what "brand drivers," or values and aspects of the brand, were consistently appreciated in all areas. They then determined the best positioning and character with which to present the brand so as to play to those strengths and move the brand toward its desired future.

The challenge for AT&T was to redefine its brand character in a way that would help lead it forward, without abandoning its past (see old logo below left, new logo below right).

The rollout of the updated identity included store and trade-show environments, a global packaging program, and extensive internal training to make everyone in the organization familiar with the thinking behind the new look. All these efforts are constantly checked to see if customers are indeed connecting the new brand character with the desired traits, and adjusted if necessary.

Barclays

Interbrand helped Barclays to develop the visual identity of the 300-year-old institution and create a fresh tone of voice to reflect a new positioning that aimed to change traditional perceptions of large financial services organizations. When it came time to rally the bank's 5,000 employees behind the new positioning, visual identity, and tone of voice, Interbrand undertook an internal campaign that "celebrates the inventive spirit of the brand and its people."

The campaign launch was timed to signal Barclays' move to new headquarters at London's Canary Wharf, to instill pride in employees, and to raise awareness of Barclays among the millions of commuters who pass through one of London's busiest stations each day. Posters in and around the Canary Wharf tube station engaged passersby through tongue-in-cheek claims about what makes Barclays people special, and what makes non-Barclays people not so special. The posters used a mixture of typography and photography, combined with a confident, witty tone of voice. This idea was carried across internal items including coffee mugs, postcards, and directional signage, making it clear to staff that they are valued.

Barclays people are more romantic.
(Because great ideas make our hearts skip a beat.)

BARCLAYS
Now there's a thought

Barclays people smell nicer.
(Because great ideas come to us in the shower.)

BARCLAYS
Now there's a thought

← Heron Quays DLR ⊖   ⊖ Canary Wharf DLR →

Could the last one out, please turn off the lights?

Sharp-tongued.
Lacks warmth.
Prone to hissy fitsss.
Not like a Barclays person.

clays people
better singers.

BARCLAYS

Irving's work is deceptive. It has the delicacy and passion for minute detail that one expects from a small creative shop, when in fact the agency is a fairly large one. Its work seems at first glance simple, almost undesigned, when in fact it is the result of great deliberation, careful research, and diligent craftsmanship. Understatement is often a sign of refinement and exclusivity, and that's just what many of Irving's clients strive for.

Irving's designs reflect the passion for fine quality and distinction that typifies its clients' brands. While the principals, Julian Roberts and Mark Brown, have extensive backgrounds in fashion and retail, they are equally at home working with identity, print, and packaging designs for food, hospitality, and gifts.

Many of Irving's designs hark back to an earlier age of craftsmanship. Their spare, clean approach speaks clearly to customers looking for a pure, personalized experience amid the noise and throwaway aesthetic of the digital age. Above all, Irving's work invites the customer to linger and savor the benefits of the brand, emphasizing the wholesomeness and value of each piece.

The Fine Cheese Co.

The Fine Cheese Co., a quintessentially English brand, has become a global hit, from Tokyo to New York. Acting as brand guardians for the last decade, Irving has created and developed a distinctive design language which reflects both the origins and the artisanal philosophy of the brand.

From one small retail outlet in Bath, The Fine Cheese Co. originally started out as a cheese retailer and wholesaler. To help grow the business, Irving has worked hand in hand with the brand's founders to develop a range of retail products to partner and complement cheese, from crackers through to pickles. The products are now sold in the world's best food stores and delicatessens including Dean & Deluca in New York and The Park Hyatt in Tokyo, through to Fortnum & Mason in London.

Along with packaging, Irving also develop all the sales and marketing collateral for the brand, including their mail-order catalogs and exhibition stands.

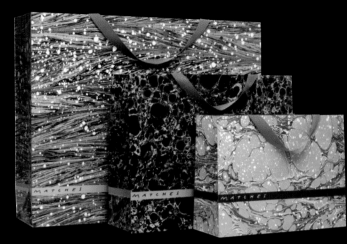

Matches

Matches are a true fashion innovator with global recognition. A series of unique stores and an inspirational approach to men's and women's fashion have placed it at the heart of fashionistas across Europe, The Middle East, and the US.

Irving work with Matches to create a seasonally shifting identity, packaging, and communications. Store environments reflect Matches unconventional aesthetic: handcrafted, vintage, and glamourous elements are combined to create a unique experience in each store that reflects the fashion aspirations of the Matches customer. Irving were also tasked with developing a range of packaging that would create an iconic statement. The designers worked with paper-marbling specialist Ann Muir to create a one-off series of papers, patterns, and colorways. Fabric handles were dyed to work with the papers, and flat-pack, self-sealing boxes with integral magnetic

Fiona Cairns

Irving was asked to create a logo that reflected the skill and craftsmanship of cakemaker Fiona Cairns. They worked with calligrapher Peter Horridge to create an identity with style—the flourishes symbolize ribbons, which come together at the top of the logotype to form a "cake."

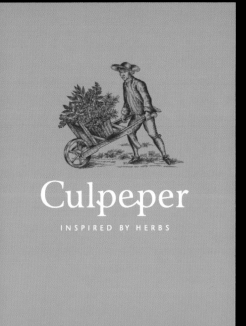

Culpeper

Culpeper specializes in producing and selling a range of lifestyle products inspired by herbs, from bath and skincare products to food and comestibles. In 2005, Irving was asked to redesign the identity for a relaunch of Culpeper products into new stores. The custom font is a contemporary reflection of seventeenth-century typography, while the pen-and-ink illustration portrays the inspiration for the brand—Nicholas Culpeper with a barrow of fresh herbs.

Lippincott Mercer

One of the oldest agencies in the branding business today, Lippincott Mercer traces its roots to the 1940s. The founders, J. Gordon Lippincott and Walter Margulies, began, as Lippincott & Margulies, by providing product and package design to US companies. Its earliest clients included Walgreens drug stores, FTD florists, Tucker automobiles, and Waterman pens.

In the 1950s the firm was a pioneer of the discipline of corporate identity, convincing clients that planning and managing their brand's visual assets consistently—especially in international operations—could yield impressive results. Throughout the 1950s, 1960s, and 1970s, the firm continued to create logos and identities for major corporations, a large number of which are still in use today, testament to the timeless quality of the designs. Others, although now retired, are reminders of the iconic status those brands had when they were current.

In 1986 the firm was acquired by Marsh & McLennan, the professional services group whose Mercer Management Consulting division was an early leader in the application of rigorous measurement and management techniques to the field of marketing. Among the corporations that benefited from these services were American Express and Continental Airlines.

Over the years, Mercer has applied advanced economic theories to brand management, gaining valuable insights into how brands shift market demand, how changes in brand architecture affect value, and how much companies can benefit financially from improving the customer experience.

In 2003 another merger resulted in a new name—Lippincott Mercer. The firm's offerings range from strategy and consulting to brand elements such as naming and logo design, retail environments, and other aspects of the customer experience.

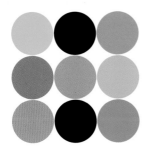

HYATT
PLACE ™

Hyatt Place

After the US hotel chain Hyatt acquired AmeriSuites, a chain of limited-service hotels, it sought to turn them into a new sub-brand of Hyatt, characterized by "a distinctive guest experience for discerning frequent travelers, with a focus on comfort and quality attuned to the traveler's needs." Lippincott Mercer developed a complete identity program including positioning, image attributes, naming, logo design, and overall hotel "vibe."

The Hyatt Place symbol is based on the idea of a "gathering place." The geometric circles come together to form a sense of place or locality. The colored dots also form the letter "H." The mark is friendly, direct, modern, and unique among the competing brands of major hotel chains.

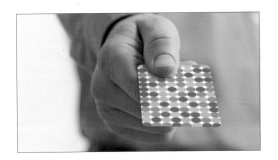

SK

SK is a conglomerate of 40 companies in South Korea. Its old identity simply consisted of the letters "S" and "K" in a nonregisterable format. Lippincott Mercer designed a new visual identity to enable SK to communicate the company's new brand positioning, and to compete as they expanded into global markets. The new logo is a combination of symbolic forms that suggests the uplifting and transformational qualities of a kite or butterfly, and the innovation of a satellite. The wings suggest a progressive nature and commitment to innovation, quality, and a growing global reach. In addition, the two wings represent the two major sources of growth within the SK Group: energy and chemicals on the one hand, and information and tele-communications on the other. The red in the logo is meant to convey the passion, energy, and dynamic qualities of SK's personality, while orange emphasizes the company's commitment to happiness and friendliness toward customers, which are the core values of the organization.

Sprint

Sprint and Nextel, two of the US's larger communications companies, merged in 2005. Sprint's broad market awareness and history of innovation made it the most appropriate choice for the brand name of the new company, yet it was important to retain the traits represented by Nextel—instant communications and entrepreneurship.

The new company recreated its logo to integrate the most valuable aspects of each constituent company's corporate identity, supporting the new brand strategy and signifying the convergence of two confident brands. Lippincott Mercer combined elements of Sprint's signature "pin drop" identity—representing clarity—and Nextel's signature palette of bold yellow and black. The new "wing" symbol reflects a sense of motion and flight, evoking the energetic, dynamic, and visionary characteristics of the new company.

The Lippincott team also produced a retail signage program for all of the company's stores, developed broad identity guidelines for use with sponsorships and business partnerships, and provided an environmental design package of banners and signs to build employee awareness and excitement for the launch of the new brand.

of advisors helping clients achieve the "prize" of their American dream. The key graphic element is a compass, symbolizing in the marketplace and built the brand essence into the company's values, corporate philanthropy initiative, and client experience.

Minale Tattersfield Design Strategy

Minale Tattersfield Design Strategy focus on helping clients lead their categories by defining and creating brands that stand out and inspire; that engage and build loyalty both internally and externally.

Their motto, "A brand is what an organization stands for," provides the starting point for distilling the rational and emotional aspects of a product or service into a single, tangible insight. A clear message of what the brand stands for can then be communicated consistently, with integrity and authenticity.

Minale Tattersfield, established in 1964, is one of the oldest privately owned branding and design agencies in the world. For over 40 years, they have been creating brands that inspire and set benchmarks for competitors. The identities created for Harrods, Eurostar, and the FA Premier League are iconic, and rank among the world's most recognized symbols of quality, service, and excellence.

Today they provide brand strategy, identity, interiors, signage, packaging, and digital communications from offices in seven countries around the world. Over the years Minale Tattersfield have received more than 300 international awards for design creativity and design effectiveness.

Although markets have become more complex, and techniques and processes have evolved, Minale Tattersfield's strengths still lie with the approach they pioneered in the early 1960s—to analyze and understand the problem first, and to allow a creative idea to develop from that.

Minale Tattersfield's work is creatively led, but strategically driven. It aims to energize and transform, to surprise and delight, to challenge convention and inspire change.

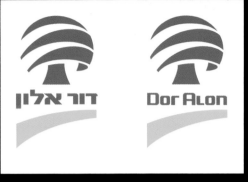

Dor Alon

Israel's second- and third-largest gasoline companies, Dor and Alon, merged and needed a new identity. The solution incorporated the three "fins" from the Dor logo and the Alon tree (alon means oak in Hebrew) into a new identity that is more dynamic and up to date than either of the previous ones.

The colors are those of the existing Alon identity, with an emphasis on the green. Materials for the station signage were specially chosen to withstand the intense sun of the Middle Eastern climate: the colors are guaranteed for 10 years.

Each filling station has two separate offerings: gasoline and food. Since these appeal to different parts of the customer's psyche, it was appropriate to take a separate design approach for each: a harder, technical engineering look for the fuel, and a softer, warmer, friendlier appeal for the food area.

Minale Tattersfield has extensive experience designing filling stations around the world, and often uses color as a device to differentiate fuel from food areas. In the case of Dor Alon, it used gentle waves in a broad palette of pastels to create an inviting atmosphere. A stylized acorn illustrates the name Alonit, which means little oak, and since the majority of Israel's population also speaks English, the bilingual pun "alon-eat" contributes to the friendly brand image

Caspian

Caspian is an Iranian company that competes throughout the Middle East region, including Afghanistan, against Western brands such as Shell, Agip, and BP's Castrol. Caspian produces and markets motor oil, lubricants, and brake fluids—a market that, given the relatively rough condition of many old cars and roads in the region, is rather vibrant!

The brand needed to present itself as the equal of its competitors in terms of quality. The new identity is notably modernized and Westernized, including the replacement of the Farsi/Arabic script with an English/Latin logo.

The aesthetic and stylish "hump," a constant feature of all products in the range, suggests improved car performance and evokes the classical Persian Sphinx shape, denoting the company's home territory. The containers are easy to hold, with excellent pouring capability, and the uppermost point of the hump acts as a load-bearing feature for stacking purposes.

Colombina

This multinational candy, chocolate, and biscuit company dates back to the 1950s, and was aware that its brand was looking old and dated. As the company had spread from its origins in Colombia to a strong presence across South America, the US, Asia, and Europe, its identity and packaging were losing touch with young consumers, and losing ground to its competitors.

The overcomplicated logo was simplified and updated, given a more dynamic form while retaining enough of its earlier self to stay recognizable. Product identities were also redesigned, and all the packaging ranges were brought together under a clear, structured "architecture" that reinforces brand recognition. In addition to an extensive corporate identity manual, Minale produced mini-manuals for each main product range.

Lollipops with the popular Bon Bon Bum (pronounced "boom") brand, for example, are sold at supermarkets, corner shops, and by street vendors. There are many flavors, with new ones developed all the time. The new branding system gives them a coordinated look to increase recognition, while still allowing creative freedom for the package designs of individual flavors.

Melinda

With this project, Minale Tattersfield succeeded in creating a strong brand for a commodity product on behalf of a client that is not an actual producer, but an organization representing thousands of independent growers around Trento in northern Italy.

The name alludes to the Italian word for apple—mela—and the apple-shaped letter M in the new logo is also suggestive of a heart. Dark blue provides a clear contrast for good legibility, while green leaves are a sign of a healthy crop. The logo is applied in the form of a little sticker on every single piece of fruit.

The branding was so successful—generating demand in new markets across Europe—that Minale was asked to extend it to new products: dried apple slices, fruit mousse, fruit juices, and fruit bars. All designs featured the logo and large images of fresh, golden apples. When the juice was launched, all 200,000 bottles from the initial production run sold out in one week.

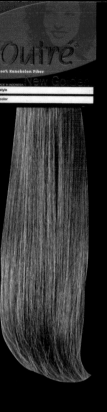

Outré

Outré is a brand of natural and artificial hair extensions marketed to black women in North America and Europe. The brand has been around since the 1980s, but was languishing "because it wasn't loved and taken care of," according to Marcello Minale. "It didn't reflect the aspirations of a young person today." Feme, the brand's owner, did research in the UK, with a view to expanding into other European countries. The strategy was to refesh the Outré identity and reposition the brand to attract a more "trendy" audience. "We wanted to make it younger, give it more bling," says Minale. "The ideal customer has an image like Beyoncé; a good girl but still streetwise." The singer Brandi is a brand spokeswoman for Sensational, Outré's sister in the US.

Minale developed a new brand architecture with five lines, each representing a different lifestyle. Each line is made from different materials and has different characteristics that are constantly updated to suit new styles and fashion trends.

The packaging was redesigned to keep production simple. The "O" in the identity plays a functional role—hair is clipped to the back of the circle and slid into a tray. Previous packaging had the hair on a generic backboard, in a plastic bag. The new design is multifunctional and allows for specific product information, such as color and length, to be stamped onto a full-color line package, saving money without sacrificing quality of presentation.

Manicure Express

Manicure Express—a name chosen to work in a multilingual environment—represents a new concept in nail care in Russia. Aimed at middle-income women who prefer to simply show up rather than make an appointment, the brand is modern and friendly, and decidedly mass-market, although outlets are located in upmarket malls, airports, and other high-traffic areas.

The colors are vibrant, to communicate quickly in cluttered environments, and the simple, European-feel graphics allow for easy extension into personal-care product ranges. The phenomenal success of me resulted in dozens of new outlets opening within the first months of operation. The brand was extended from its core offering to a line of nail-care products. A Manicure Express Deluxe version was also tested for "upmarket" office developments.

One of the surprise lessons from the first outlet, which opened in Moscow in 2006, was the unexpectedly large number of men using the service—an example of customers redefining a brand on their own terms.

Shark energy drink

This brand identity was completely reinvented for the purpose of expanding out of its original market, Thailand, where it had been packaged in medicine bottles and appealed mainly to local laborers. The exciting new logo combines name and graphic in one device, helping to make an indelible impression on its intended global youth market—with recognition assured regardless of the local language or script.

The identity was applied, with careful consistency, to a new, silver can and range of advertising and marketing materials. Sponsorship of motorcycle racing gave the brand strong visibility in a high-energy sports setting and helped ensure a high-impact rollout.

From China to Ukraine to Portugal, from Estonia to Lebanon to South Africa, Shark is now one of the top energy-drink brands in every country in which it is sold, competing well even against brands that had enjoyed a significant head start.

Building brands is a way of life for the agency founded, in 2001, by Martyn Tipping and Robert Sprung—especially when it comes to brand extensions and the "architecture" of brands and brand names. The agency teams up with *Brandweek* magazine annually to conduct a brand extension survey, in which professionals from a variety of marketing and branding disciplines rate and respond to the past year's brand-extension hits and misses. (As Robert is quick to point out, quite often the misses are more instructive than the hits.) TippingSprung's own portfolio of branding work, for big and small clients from many sectors, includes many brand extensions.

The agency is based in New York, with offices in London and Los Angeles, and offers services in strategy, naming, design, licensing, and research. Clients range from Fortune 500 companies including Avaya, GE, and Eli Lilly (featured here), to aspiring and fast-growing brands that, with a little luck and the right branding approach, could one day join the big leagues. In the case of Pinnacor and Tapestry Pharmaceuticals, TippingSprung came up with new names to reflect a change of direction in the business. Time Inc.'s Giftscriptions is a new concept for giving magazine subscriptions as a gift, Stirrings was able to expand its sales with a new name, and Tidewell Hospice's new brand identity helped customers see the organization's strengths, which had been obscured by its old name.

InnoCentive

Eli Lilly, the pharmaceuticals giant, sought to develop a brand identity for their online venture that would allow scientists and science-based companies around the world to collaborate on innovative solutions to complex challenges. TippingSprung created the name InnoCentive to communicate the key benefit of the online forum—innovative incentives. The network allows 85,000 scientists in 175 countries to solve tough research problems, and to obtain professional recognition and financial awards from companies.

Answers That Matter.

INNOCENTIVE

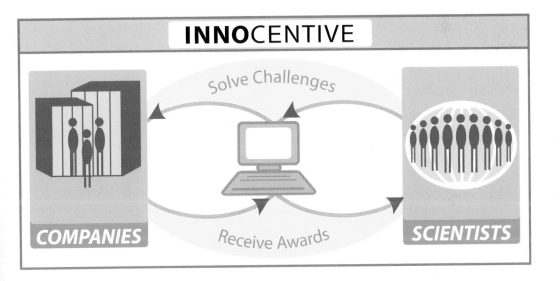

Avaya

After its spin-off from Lucent Technologies (itself a spin-off from AT&T's Bell Labs), Avaya found itself with a new name, logo, and tagline, but without a clear idea of how to communicate its new brand position to customers and employees. It was a classic case of putting the cart before the horse in the branding process.

TippingSprung carried out extensive research with Avaya's senior management, and with existing and prospective customers. The agency was then able to develop a brand positioning based on the idea of "communications-driven results."

A brand architecture was developed, as well as naming, and guidelines for the tone and manner of communications. Within two years of the new brand positioning being carried out, Avaya's market share grew to 25%, surpassing the leader, whose share had meanwhile dropped to 23% from 40%.

FIFA World Cup™ Challenge:

Provide converged communications for the world's most popular sporting event by designing, building, monitoring & maintaining a network with:

- 27 venues (20 stadiums)
- 10,000 communications devices
- 40,000 network connections
- 100,000 IP calls completed daily
- $200,000 long distance savings
- 3,200,000 IP & analog calls completed
- 99.999% error-free transmission

Challenge met:

Zero network outages, practically flawless performance

Photo Credit: Action Images/John Sibley

IP Telephony | Contact Centers | Unified Communication | Services

Stirrings

TippingSprung came up with the name Stirrings for a premium line of cocktail mixers from a company called Nantucket Offshore. The producer wanted to be at the forefront of cocktail culture, creating exciting new mixes and making it as easy to reach for a Pomegranatini at the end of the day as a glass of wine or a beer.

Stirrings later asked TippingSprung to develop the name, identity, and packaging for a new line of cocktail mixers to be sold exclusively at Target, a chain of stylish discount stores. The name they chose, Cocktail Empouria, suggests a wide range of cocktail mixers, and also combines elegance and humor. The packaging is bold, clean, and distinctive, and reinforces the idea that the mixers make it easy to enjoy great-tasting cocktails. TippingSprung also designed Cocktail Empouria gift boxes for Target.

Est. 1997, NANTUCKET

Giftscriptions

Until recently, giving the gift of a magazine subscription was an uninspiring experience for both giver and recipient. The gift-giver would run the risk that their giftee already received the magazine or, worse still, had no interest in it. And the recipient had nothing to open as a gift, except perhaps a postcard telling them they could expect to receive their first issue in eight to twelve weeks.

For the 2004 holiday season (late November to early January), Time Inc. tested a trial magazine gift subscription product in drugstores and bookstores. The Magazine Subscription Gift Pack consisted of a prepaid reply card and a list of 50 magazines in an oversize cardboard sleeve, all wrapped in cellophane. Consumers loved the idea of being able to give a gift that enabled recipients to choose their own magazine subscription, but they felt that the overall look and feel of the product left room for improvement.

Time Inc. asked TippingSprung to turn the product into a brand. Working closely with the team at Time, and supported by extensive consumer research, they defined the positioning, identity, and overall brand experience. This included creating the product format and structure, Giftscriptions identity, key communication messages, and point-of-sale presence.

The new Giftscriptions gift box was launched in time for the 2005 holiday season at retailers including Barnes & Noble, Wal-Mart, Best Buy, and Borders, to great success. The elegantly packaged product clearly communicates choice—this emerged as a key product benefit in the research. The packaging also makes it clear, to both giver and recipient, how to use the product—another important factor discovered through the research.

Thanks to the product rebranding, sales increased smartly. Based on the success of the holiday program, Time Inc. launched a special Giftscriptions for Mother's Day 2006, and introduced the brand to new retailers including Hudson News, Home Depot, Amazon.com, and Walgreens.

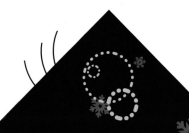

THE PERFECT
CHOICE EVERY TIME!

Giftscriptions is a new
magazine gift subscription
product that allows the recipient
to choose from 50 different
magazine subscriptions. Time Inc. chose
TippingSprung to bring the Giftscriptions
brand to life, from positioning, naming, and product
structure, all the way through to packaging
design and creation of PoP displays. >>

You can find Giftscriptions
at Barnes & Noble, Wegmans,
Walmart, BestBuy, Borders, and
Books-A-Million. And you can find
TippingSprung at 212.268.4800
or online at tippingsprung.com.

 tipping sprung

Tidewell

Research showed that the Hospice of Southwest Florida was mistakenly seen by key target audiences as the local branch of a national hospice movement, rather than an independent, not-for-profit organization. The challenge for TippingSprung was to build a brand for Hospice that would serve as a rallying point for patients and their families, as well as employees, donors, and community physicians.

TippingSprung came up with the name Tidewell, and tested it with people aged between 60 and 80, and among physicians. The results of this research proved the name to be memorable and distinctive, while motivating respondents to learn more about the organization. The distinctive Tidewell logotype, also developed by TippingSprung, is organic and soothing, and supports the organization's focus on building relationships. The new Tidewell brand, launched in 2005, was received enthusiastically by employees and the local community alike.

Tapestry Pharmaceuticals

NaPro BioTherapeutics was established in 1991 as a pharmaceutical company focusing on the chemistry of natural products. By 2004 the company had changed its focus to developing proprietary therapies for the treatment of cancer, and felt that its old corporate name was no longer relevant or appropriate.

TippingSprung developed the name Tapestry Pharmaceuticals to suggest the strands of DNA that are the focus of the company's genetic research. The name also suggests the complex and interdisciplinary nature of pharmaceutical drug development. In a category that is crowded with similar-sounding names ("Gen," "Cell," "Bio," and "Tech"), Tapestry stands out as contemporary and memorable.

mong designers, Pentagram enjoys one of he finest reputations in the world. It began 1972 as a cooperative of five independent esigners, hence the name. Further offices pened in New York in 1978, San Francisco 1986, Austin in 1994, and Berlin in 2002. lthough Pentagram now includes some 9 partners across the globe, its independent artnership structure and small-firm ethos ave remained remarkably intact.

Pentagram's work is usually thought f in terms of design rather than branding. covers a wide variety of design areas, rom product design to graphic design, oftware interfaces to environmental esign, book design to signage, and many ther niche fields. Inevitably, however, nce one begins to think of Pentagram's or any designer's) work through the lens f branding, it starts to make sense that should be seen that way. Design is one of ne pillars of brand building, and it is virtually npossible to design anything without it eing part of the brand at some level.

In many ways, a designer approaches the hallenges of his or her work in the same vay that one should approach branding: boking for the insight at the heart of the natter, searching for bright ideas to embody hat insight, and drawing on a vocabulary f visual and sensory cues, both universal and culturally specific, to convey those deas with a compelling immediacy.

What characterizes much of Pentagram's work is the intelligence and apparent effortlessness of many of its solutions, along with its ability to cross over styles and genres. But their simplicity is deceiving— many of the designs Pentagram has produced have stood the test of time and are widely recognized as timeless, iconic, and simply enjoyable to look at.

The Dana Centre

The Dana Centre is the only venue of its kind in the UK. It is dedicated to eating, drinking, talking, and performing science. It deliberately sets out to challenge the notion that science is a solemn, serious business. This is a place where scientists come face-to-face with members of the public on equal terms. Here, everyone can express their opinions and ideas on the big scientific issues of the day, and their cultural impact. But it's not about sitting and listening respectfully to the delivery of scientific papers. The intention is for people to talk, to argue, to experiment with ideas, to be provocative, radical, even playful.

From the reception area that bombards visitors with thought-provoking questions to the vast expanse of glass covered in a mosaic of type—a patchwork of ideas, opinions, and snatches of virtual dialogue— no one will ever be lost for words here.

Harry Pearce designed the identity with his firm Lippa Pearce before joining Pentagram in 2006. The identity, including interior and exterior graphics and signage, is wonderfully tactile, based around the concept of language, and evolving throughout the whole building. "… the space is brought to life through typography. The Dana Centre is essentially about conversation which is summed up by the great glass wall, with textual interplay running through both sides of the glass."

EAT.

EAT. was founded in 1996 as a small, family-run company devoted to selling good, simple food and drink at reasonable prices. Today it has over 70 outlets across the UK.

Pentagram partner Angus Hyland was appointed to evolve the existing identity and redefine the EAT. brand experience. This prompted a thorough investigation of the market and the credible points of differentiation between EAT. and its competitors. Based on this, a core insight was developed to guide the identity work.

The proposition highlighted the honesty at the heart of EAT.'s business—it is owned by people who have a passion for real food and drink. Communication of the proposition was achieved by developing a new logotype and design language, with guidelines for its correct and consistent use across all visual and tangible elements of the brand.

Pentagram developed an all-encompassing identity. The new logotype uses a bold, sans-serif typeface (Akzidenz Grotesk) that communicates the warmth and quality of

the brand with a distinct, contemporary tone. This bold typographical language has been combined with a color palette of warm, natural brown hues, with a range of vibrant minor colors for typography and detailing across food packaging, menu boards, and other collateral.

Graphic implementation was rolled out across each one of EAT.'s outlets by Jules Bigg at Fresh Produce, who further developed the language of the Pentagram schematic design concept and applied it to a wide range of packaging, print, and marketing materials.

ESPA

ESPA offers an unusual combination of spa-inspired products, treatments, and services that combine the very best of ancient and modern therapies with the finest-quality ingredients and skincare advances. From an extensive range of skincare treatments and oils to wraps and body polishes, ESPA products are about evoking emotion and providing a total experience of well-being for the individual.

The ESPA philosophy is about treating an individual's lifestyle in a holistic and versatile way, rediscovering one's natural balance with products and treatments that work on both emotional and physical levels. Its visual identity has been distinctive since its launch in the 1990s, but as the brand became more international, it needed to evolve the packaging to ensure better synergy between the product range and the constantly developing spa environments.

The new, classical, and timeless identity developed by Pentragram partner Domenic Lippa exudes boldness and confidence, reflecting the quality of the brand. The soft use of the color claret reflects the sensory nature of ESPA, while the delicate use of embossing and a luxury material—granite—for the packaging gives it a sense of integrity and reflects the brand's history. The new packaging design needed to create a sense of intrigue and surprise, but to keep what is special and unique about ESPA. The elements and core beliefs at the heart of the brand are reflected in the logo and the identity as a whole, which embraces a feeling of discovery and innovation.

and accessories, traces its roots to 1892, but it wasn't until the 1980s that the firm really took off, becoming one of the first chains in Britain to leave downtown locations for edge-of-town, big-box stores that offered more space and easier parking.

Several acquisitions, changes of ownership, and continued expansion led to the need for an identity that would help the brand reassure its customers about its consistency of product and service.

Halfords enjoyed a couple of rare luxuries for a retailer—a clearly defined customer base, and no direct major competitor—but this didn't guarantee the brand immunity from broader changes in its consumer base. Halfords' traditional market among do-it-yourself car enthusiasts was shrinking, for example, but in its place new opportunities were arising, based more on the experiences that wheeled life and leisure have to offer.

The new identity evolved over time. The first step was for Lippa Pearce, whose partners joined Pentagram in 2006, to build Halfords' own-brand presence in stores using packaging that worked better in terms of both visual appeal and practical use. One early achievement, developed with Kenneth Grange at Pentagram, was a series of plastic oil containers with built-in handles and a more practical shape. It was a logical next step to work on a major rethinking of the retail environment. The consultants worked with three very different interior designers in devising a variety of new store concepts to test how far the brand's dynamics could stretch without losing credibility.

nightclub interiors, used bare metal and bright graphics reminiscent of motorway signs. It had a positive impact, especially among male shoppers. The other concepts were less radical, but all ultimately informed the design of the new stores, with aspects of each surviving in different parts of the stores, which were more clearly identified to appeal to particular customer groups.

As store redesigns got under way, Halfords introduced additional services to apply across all areas, and staff training was improved. The aim was to let customers know they were dealing with specialists who shared their passions. Nevertheless, customers tended to go into the new-look stores, gasp in admiration, but not appreciate the depth of the change, so Lippa Pearce was asked to devise a new corporate identity to complete the makeover. The designers came back with the solution—"Halfords" in bold black letters on an orange background, with the "o" skewed to look like cartoon-style speeding wheels. The bold colors and typography are effective in a variety of applications.

The new identity was promoted through Halfords' sponsorship of the British Touring Car Championship, which built awareness and perceptions of Halfords as a leading brand that is enthusiastic about all aspects of motoring.

Saks Fifth Avenue

In 2004 Saks, the upmarket New York retailer, approached Pentagram to design a new identity for their stores with a graphic program that would encompass signage, advertising, direct mail, an online presence, and, most importantly, packaging.

The leadership at Saks were looking for something that would be ubiquitous and iconic—immediately identifiable when glimpsed across a busy street. Saks had never had a signature color like the famous robin-egg blue of Tiffany; nor did it have a signature pattern like the Burberry plaid. An examination of Saks' branding history showed that the store had used dozens of logos. However, many of these were variations on the same theme—cursive writing. Of these, one stood out—a logo drawn by Tom Carnese in 1973. In many people's minds, this still was the Saks logo. By coincidence, Michael Bierut, a partner at Pentagram, knew it well: it was at the heart of the identity system designed by his first boss, Massimo Vignelli.

Saks was happy to emphasize its heritage, but eager to signal that it was looking to the future. The exciting solution took the cursive logo, redrew it with the help of font designer Joe Finocchiaro, and placed it in a black square. This square was subdivided into a grid of 64 smaller "tiles" that can be shuffled and rotated to form an almost infinite number of variations. Most of the tiles, attractive in their own right, include details that reflect the graphic character of the logo entire. Enlarged, they have an energy and drama that contrasts nicely with the original mark from which they are taken.

The advantage of the identity is that it creates recognizable consistency without sameness, and the logo elements can be used in signage, direct mail, and advertising. Most importantly, there are over 40 different packages in the program, from jewelry boxes to hat boxes, and four sizes of shopping bag. No two are alike, yet they all go together. The hope is that shoppers will associate them with the style and elan of Saks Fifth Avenue.

Oskar: Retail experience

Design by Enterprise IG

Established in 2000, Oskar faced an uphill battle as the third cell-phone operator to enter the market in the Czech Republic. Nonetheless, the strong, friendly, local personality of the brand made an indelible impression on the minds of Czech consumers, who voted it most dynamic Czech company in a 2004 survey.

However, the retail experience was one area in which Oskar was not living up to its brand promise or values. The brief to Enterprise IG was to create an experience for Oskar's shops that was challenging, captivating, respectful, and inspiring.

Enterprise IG was given only six months to deliver a concept that would work across flagship and main-street stores, kiosks, and mobile units. The solution needed to improve the retail experience, while bringing the Oskar personality and brand values to life. The store design had to give people a strong sense of freedom and control—key features of Oskar's positioning.

Enterprise started by developing a rich and distinctive design language for Oskar. This language used different elements and materials to engage consumers. Each store contained a real tree, a surprising and delightful embodiment of the brand's ethos of vitality and growth, supported by a firm root and branch network. The interiors contrasted soft and padded materials with hard elements such as solid surfacing to stimulate the senses.

Bringing to life the Oskar claim, customers were invited to "speak their mind" in each store by writing or drawing on a backlit "self-expression wall." Customers were also free to explore the interfaces of phones, which were left on custom-built browsing seating. Functional improvements were also made. A new queuing system was devised to free people to explore the store while waiting for service; instead of numbers, they were given characters. Enterprise IG also designed a more effective storage system and pods that combined cash desks with interactive self-help tools, giving customers, rather than staff, a sense of ownership.

All these elements were designed in kit form so that they could be mixed and matched with the retail environment, whether a store, a kiosk, or a mobile "Oskaravan" bringing Oskar to customers in areas outside major towns.

Customer research indicated a very positive response to the store experience, which cemented the brand benefits in customers' minds. A number of additional stores were opened in 2004 and 2005. Though the Oskar brand was later replaced by that of Vodafone, the key elements of the store environment were retained.

Retail experience

The retail chain for Oskar had to emphasize the quirky, energetic characteristics that made it different from its two larger competitors. Design features included self-service stations, a live tree, and a wall on which customers could write messages.

Horizon Fitness: Product rebranding

Design by Hanson Dodge Creative

A brand needs strong fundamentals— quality, design, durability—in order to work, but many products with strong fundamentals lack an effective brand identity to help them make the most of these strengths when it comes to winning and keeping customers, and being able to charge a strong price.

Horizon Fitness, a multinational maker of exercise equipment, is a good case in point. Their products were good, but customer perception of them could have been better. The brand was lagging behind its fundamentals.

Hanson Dodge—a design and branding agency committed to brands centered around an active lifestyle—rose to the challenge. Through targeted brand development, disciplined brand management, breakthrough design, and smart strategies for the sales channel, Hanson Dodge was able to help Horizon Fitness pump up its leadership position in the highly competitive fields of sporting goods and specialty sports retail.

After all the research, analysis, and strategy development, work began on the development of a visual identity.

The elements—logo, typography, visual style, tone of voice—needed to be carefully crafted to reflect both the technical merits of the product and the athletic aspirations of the customer.

Next, the products had to be arranged and styled for photography (and the photos retouched) in just the right way. Angles, lighting, and details such as highlights on the textured treadmill had to be perfect. Illustrations of the inner mechanics were made to show the advantages from a technical standpoint, in a style compatible with the photography. Finally, a series of outdoor and studio images of people running, exercising, and working out was made to complement the product shots, and to bring an emotional element to the communications.

The visual materials, along with texts expertly rewritten in a lucid and precise, yet friendly voice, were assembled into a series of interactive training materials, catalogs, brochures, and customer websites.

The end result is a strong brand that properly reflects the strengths of the products. Its quality and consistency in all details has been rewarded with wide recognition and double-digit sales increases.

Printed collateral

A carefully crafted image is maintained across printed materials such as product brochures and magazine advertisements. Every detail is attended to: illustration, photography, color palette, logo, typography, graphic elements, layout, and tone of writing. All elements work in harmony to convey a unified impression of the values and qualities of the product.

Brand standards

Many brand identities have to be implemented by people outside the company. These people need to be made familiar with all the different design elements, such as logo, color, and typography, and how best to use them. A manual offers a handy reference to answer the question, "How should this look?"

LOGO: THE HEART OF THE BRAND

The Horizon Fitness logo appears on everything from corporate communications and the Web to on-product point of sale and decals. To maintain the integrity of the brand, it needs to be used consistently and appropriately in all places.

E. Minimum size

VERTICAL LOGO ORIENTATION
Use the vertical logo when space is primarily vertical or rectangular.

HORIZONTAL LOGO ORIENTATION
Use the horizontal logo when compositions only provide long, narrow areas for the logo (e.g. Web headers and banners, document footers, vertical banners).

COOL AND SLEEK: THE BRAND COLORS

TRADE GOTHIC: THE BRAND TYPEFACE

ABCDEFGHIJKLMNOPQRSTUVWXYZ
abcdefghijklmnopqrstuvwxyz123456789

ABCDEFGHIJKLMNOPQRSTUVWXYZ
abcdefghijklmnopqrstuvwxyz123456789

ABCDEFGHIJKLMNOPQRSTUVWXYZ
abcdefghijklmnopqrstuvwxyz123456789

ABCDEFGHIJKLMNOPQRSTUVWXYZ
abcdefghijklmnopqrstuvwxyz123456789

ABCDEFGHIJKLMNOPQRSTUVWXYZ
abcdefghijklmnopqrstuvwxyz123456789

SCIENCE, SIMPLIFIED: TECH BRANDS

ERGOflow

COMFORTzone

INstep

SUPERconductor

QUIETdrive

STABLEframe

FeatherLIGHT

SMARTboard

BREAKING DOWN THE TECH BRAND LOGOTYPE

COMFORTzone™

The best deck under your feet.

GETTING ATTENTION: HEADLINE TYPE STYLE

EX-44
The total elliptical experience.

LIFESTYLE PHOTOGRAPHY

Models

Environment & Lighting

Action & Propping

PRODUCT PHOTOGRAPHY

2007 HORIZON SERIES PRODUCT CATALOG

Treadmills vs. Ellipticals.

ONLINE & IN TOUCH: HORIZON SERIES WEB SITE

HORIZON SERIES WEB SITE, CONTINUED

Lago di Garda: Place rebranding

Design by Minale Tattersfield
Design Strategy

The towns and countryside on the shores of Lake Garda are among Italy's top tourist destinations. Research has confirmed that the area contains all the best Italy has to offer in microcosm: history, culture, fresh fruit and vegetables, food and wine, and water recreation that rivals any coastal resort. The steady wind, known as the Torbola, that descends from the Alpine valleys makes Garda a world-renowned windsurfing spot. The only problem is that Garda falls across three of Italy's provinces—Trentino, Lombardia, and Veneto—and there was little coordination between them in marketing the delights of Garda to the world. Each presented a different message, diluting the impact of their efforts.

But a solution became readily apparent, and at once made working for three clients more manageable. The new logo uses five colors, with a silhouetted icon in each color to show off the many attractions of Garda. The luxury of using five colors in the logo was made possible by the fact that each region was happy to see the colors of its own identity incorporated in the solution, and by the assurance that full-color graphics would be possible on every application.

Communicating place
Lago di Garda captures all that is best about Italy in one compact region, and its new identity needed to reflect that: historic castles, sailing and windsurfing, olive growing, fine wine, and sandy beaches.

Consistent application
The logo developed by Minale Tattersfield turns each letter of the name into an icon for one of Garda's varied attractions. Each color reinforces its symbol, forming a pleasing whole that evokes the entire spectrum of offerings. A brand manual specifies how the identity should be applied consistently to various things, including personnel uniforms.

Visual style
The Garda identity is more than just a logo: for example, it includes directions on how to use images to create a visual style that conveys the brand appropriately.

Florida Blue: Brand extension

Design by Infinia

Blue Cross and Blue Shield of Florida is the foremost provider of health insurance in the State, a fixture in its communities for over half a century. Florida Blue marks the company's first foray into retail. The prototype store launched in the city of Jacksonville, and, although it may seem a major leap to start selling health insurance over the counter, the extension remains strategically consistent with their brand and its current expression, "How can Blue help you?" Consequently, all the branding work Infinia created reflects, in both content and expression, a more human, more engaging voice. The aim of the store is to make planning and purchasing health insurance more understandable and less intimidating.

The need to simplify what is complex guided the choice of textual and visual vocabulary: conversational, directional language balancing symbolic illustration, and the elevation of the square store logo into the design as "the Blue box." From the storefront to the interior, to the print ads, radio commercials, outdoor billboards, and promotional events, the tone is one of empathy, engagement, and welcome, complementing and signaling the informal, yet informational experience that visitors can expect.

In addition to speaking with an agent, customers can serve themselves, attend seminars, and get information about health-related community activities and programs. Florida Blue is more than just a place to shop for policies—it is also an opportunity for the organization to get closer to its customers, learn about their needs, and get a better understanding of the issues they face.

The brand extension is about accessibility, plain-speaking dialogue, and simplicity. It is an antidote to faceless call centers and endless online trawling for information— a place where people can get the answers they've been looking for, face-to-face.

Store facade
The transparency of the Florida Blue store facade reflects the brand's openness and accessibility, while silhouettes emphasize the human aspect that Florida Blue brings to the process of choosing health insurance in person.

Reception area
The interior conveys clarity, simplicity, and engagement: a welcoming reception area is backed by a supergraphic of the Florida Blue mission, with convenient dispensers for collateral material such as brochures and reports.

Office layout
Low-walled workspaces and vivid, easily navigable wall displays combine the informal with the informational.

Mini Cooper: Brand revival

Design by Interbrand

The Mini Cooper first appeared in 1959—a diminutive, affordable, and very British little car. It quickly became a cult classic, famous for an appeal that transcended class, even though the Mini was not known for quality or reliability. When BMW acquired the rights to the brand and approached Interbrand for the relaunch in 2001, it was clear that the new Mini Cooper brand would have to be developed with a fresh approach. Embracing the rich history and cult status of the brand was critical: the revived brand would have to evoke feelings and experience as much as the car itself.

Through in-depth research, Interbrand uncovered the core insight of the Mini brand: a passion for excitement. By further defining excitement, they were able to name three key pillars of the brand—extroversion, spontaneity, and chicness.

These pillars informed all aspects of the brand, from verbal to visual, including the unique notion of "inside the box." This idea stemmed from the days of the cult Matchbox cars; kids and adults collected and displayed mini versions of their favorite cars. The excitement of what was "inside the box" combined with the notion of the car as a work of art led to the Mini frame, which complemented the irreverent tone of voice in all media.

The branding has been irreverent while remaining consistent to the brand attributes and product benefits. This combination has resulted in a new generation of enthusiasts, giving the revived brand a new life.

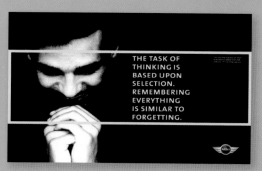

Brand insight

The strength of the old Mini lay in its quirkiness and ability to connote excitement which, perhaps uniquely among car brands, transcended class. The strength of the new Mini lies in Interbrand having identified this insight and exploited it through an irreverent, exuberant identity that gives a nod to the cult classic and redefines it for new generations.

Consistent brand character

The colored frame, with its strong allusion to brand character, provides a handy and eye-catching way to tie ad campaigns, media materials, and showroom presentations together.

Carluccio's: Storytelling

Design by Irving

When you step into a Carluccio's, whether for a full meal at one of the Caffés around the UK, to buy a jar of their exquisite wild fennel sauce, or to order another box of gianduiotti from the website, you are stepping into the passion and expertise of Antonio and Priscilla Carluccio, whose knowledge of regional Italian food and producers is a result of their extensive travels in Italy. Their lifelong passion for the food of Italy is the basis for an equally passionate brand.

The identity, packaging, communication, and interiors of each location all reflect the sense of delight and surprise that customers share with Antonio and Priscilla. Carluccio's stands for zest without overdoing things; for traditional quality in a contemporary, joyful environment.

Visual style

It's difficult to pin down what it is that defines Carluccio's visual style, and that's what makes it so intriguing. Whether it's a simple label on a jar of antipasto, the fancy woodcuts on a box of gianduiotti or panettone, the tissue-paper wrapping on a tartufo dolce, or the lettering draped around an impossibly slender bottle of balsamic vinegar, the elegant, distinctive typography communicates a refined taste and sensory satisfaction.

The images and color schemes used avoid the clichés of Italy. Neither does Carluccio's adhere to a fixed set of brand identity guidelines. Instead, the graphics and environments are designed in a spirit of spontaneity and intuitive feeling for the right typefaces and colors. The result is an astute hybrid of inherently Italian stylishness, and a visual playfulness that is typically English.

The brand is a paean to good taste that transcends cultural borders and pleases the visual palette as much as the oral one.

Menus and communications
The approach that works so well for packaging also works for printed items like menus, leaflets, posters, and invitations: clear, understated typography makes a strong, silent statement about the brand values and promises.

Décor and interior design
Interior design by Design
LSM. The visual style of the
brand is carried over into the
décor of the café interiors,
as well as their signage. This
creates a holistic experience
of the brand, from the moment
a customer enters the space
until long after they take the
product home to enjoy.

IEEE: Naming

Design by TippingSprung

"It is remarkable how often we get asked to duplicate the 'Intel Inside' effect, in order to brand some proprietary technology in a memorable way," says Robert Sprung, one of the principals of TippingSprung. "Given the tremendous success, and marketing budget, of the Intel program, this is akin to asking a designer to 'give me something like the Nike swoosh.'"

The branding of standards is a clear trend, particularly in the area of high technology. Helping to lead the way in this area is the Institute of Electrical and Electronics Engineers, known as IEEE (pronounced Eye-triple-E), one of the oldest and most respected standards organizations in the world, and one of TippingSprung's clients. In the past, standards developed by IEEE were successfully marketed with brands created by third parties such as Intel (Centrino) and the Wi-Fi Alliance.

How does a branded standard benefit the organization that developed it, the company that makes and markets a product adhering to it, and the consumer? The answers offer lessons not only in the branding of technology, but also in the branding of all "ingredients," from high-tech products to food.

Until Wi-Fi Alliance came up with the name Wi-Fi, the standard for short-range wireless communication between computers and modems was simply called IEEE 802.11™— hardly something to roll off the tongue at a cocktail party. A consortium of several dozen technology companies joined Wi-Fi Alliance in 1999. It handles testing, certification, and licensing, and has branded over 1,500 products with the Wi-Fi name. The money earned from these activities goes to the Alliance and its labs, rather than to IEEE.

Something very similar happened with WiMAX (built on IEEE 802.16™), Centrino (based on IEEE 802.11™, but completely

MOBILE TECHNOLOGY

LIVIUM™

◆ IEEE

intertwined in the public mind with Intel products), and FireWire (from which IEEE 1394™ was developed).

By developing its own brands for its own standards, IEEE would not only be able to share the value of its work, it could also help companies building products to IEEE standards differentiate themselves in the market. At the same time, it would help IEEE strengthen its own brand and maintain greater control over its licensing, preventing brands from being "subdivided" by licensees.

With IEEE 1625™ a standard for rechargeable computer batteries, the organization turned to TippingSprung to come up with a name and brand identity. Martyn Tipping, Director of Brand Strategy at TippingSprung, worked closely with IEEE and, after a rigorous process, 1625 was reborn as Livium: a reference to the Lithium-Ion technology that also implies

"live" power. International testing confirmed that "Livium" is easily understandable, appropriate in key languages other than English, and able to be trademarked around the world.

Household names
As technology standards become part of everyday conversation, brand names like Centrino, FireWire, and Wi-Fi help customers discuss and remember them, and promote confidence in the products. TippingSprung developed the Livium brand name and visual identity for the laptop battery standard IEEE 1625.

Glossary

While I have made a strenuous effort to avoid branding jargon in this book—I feel plain English is always preferable—there are some key terms and concepts, that readers may want to refer to, and have succinctly defined.

alignment
This occurs when all the elements of brand identity are properly coordinated in support of the brand insight. A brand is said to be out of alignment when its parts don't function as a sensible whole that backs up the ideas the brand should be embodying.

alternative marketing
The use of unconventional media and technology strategies to communicate a brand message and raise interest in a brand, or the use of social networking mechanisms to generate viral campaigns; most commonly, online promotional activities and word-of-mouth campaigns aim at generating brand buzz.

avatar
See logo

brand
A tangible, symbolic system created by a producer to evoke an intangible notion in a customer's mind. The system comprises a discrete identity—name, logo, color, visual style, tone of voice, product design, package design, advertising, approach to customer service, and environmental design—associated with an insight involving rational product benefits, emotional desires, and personal aspirations.

brand ambassador
Any person representing a brand in one of two functions: getting people interested in the brand, or maintaining loyalty (e.g. through customer service) after they have bought the brand.

brand architecture
A conceptual structure of brands, sub-brands, and co-brands from the same producer that provides a useful tool for clarifying their hierarchy and relationships. Often the components of a brand's architecture are aimed at particular customer groups or market segments. (Also called brand portfolio.)

brand assets
The most readily recognizable elements of a brand, for example a color that is widely recognized as "belonging" to the brand; also the ideas associated with a brand in customers' minds, for example a widely shared perception of quality.

brand equity
The value that resides in a brand, thanks to its familiarity to large numbers of people, including customers, employees, the general public, and other stakeholders such as vendors, lenders, shareholders, regulatory authorities, and business partners. Brand equity can be measured as customer likeliness to buy a product bearing the brand at a certain premium.

brand experience
The sum of all of the cognitive associations a customer enjoys when coming into contact with a brand, whether visual, sensory, or emotional. Ideally, the experience should be coherent across all touchpoints, that is, all the products, marketing materials, interactions, and environments related to the brand.

brand extension
Applying a brand to a new product or service category. Different from a line extension which involves adding varieties within the same category (like flavors of ice cream), or brand licensing, in which a popular brand, especially in the field of entertainment, is applied to a generic product such as a souvenir, accessory, or toy.

brand insight
The core notion upon which a brand is built. The most powerful insights deal with the human need for self-actualization and fulfillment. A famous example is Nike's slogan "Just do it," which isn't directly related to running shoes, but rather to athletes' desire to push themselves to greater heights of achievement.

brand licensing
See brand extension

brand management
The job of ensuring that brand insights remain constantly valid, while the symbols that evoke them evolve to ensure a consistent, integral experience in the face of changing customer perceptions. The person or team doing this job is called the brand steward; the older term brand manager refers to one who manages sales and marketing functions, such as pricing or distribution, for a given brand.

brand portfolio
See brand architecture

brand steward
See brand management

brand strategy
The effort or process of bringing a brand and its development in line with business objectives. (Most brand strategy suffers from ignoring the notion that business objectives should flow from brand insight, not the other way round.)

branded house
See house of brands

branding
The process of systematically pairing a deliberately crafted, symbolic identity with insights to arouse and then satisfy expectations. May involve the determination or definition of those insights; nearly always involves the creative development of the identity.

brief
The definition of goals, with parameters like starting point, procedure, and budget, for a project in design, advertising, marketing, or branding.

buzz
What people are saying about a brand. Buzz can be influenced, but tends to operate in defiance of overt advertising and marketing. Used to be called reputation.

claim
A few words, usually presented with the logo, that express or allude to the brand insight in a memorable way. (Also called tagline, strapline, slogan.)

code

A convention, archetype, or common symbolic association exploited by a brand to establish itself more deeply in the customer's mind. A code can be motivated, that is, deliberately constructed and pushed by the brand's producer, or arbitrary, that is, picked up organically in the marketplace through popular response to a brand.

commodity

An unbranded product or service. Products or services with very weak brands are unable to charge a premium over the commodity price.

corporate identity

The brand of a company or organization, and especially its visual elements, as distinct from the brands of the products or services that it provides.

cult brand

A brand whose followers are not only highly loyal and feel a strong affinity to other fans of the brand, but also spend time and energy evangelizing, or spreading their passion for the brand to others. Commonly cited examples include Apple, Harley-Davidson, and Starbucks Coffee.

design

The act or process of giving something a deliberate form or appearance, often with aesthetic aims as well as utilitarian considerations. Different from style, which involves applying a genre-like appearance to something, often superficially. Design is a critical part of branding, because it informs most of the elements of the customer's experience, such as the form of the product and packaging, the appearance of marketing materials, the atmospherics of a shop interior, and so on.

destination branding

Defining a brand and giving a coherent identity to a place people want to visit, whether a nation, city, or resort. *See also* nation branding.

endorsement

The placement of one brand (or master brand) alongside another to lend it credibility or desirability.

generic brand

A brand belonging to a retail store (chain), generally with a label applied to a product made by a commodity manufacturer, usually sold at a lower price than major or independent brands. (Also called store brand or private label.)

house of brands vs. branded house

Procter & Gamble is an example of the former; they sell goods under individual brands like Gillette, Pampers, and Crest, but not under the house name Procter & Gamble. The Coca-Cola Company is an example of the latter; the corporation bears the name of the flagship brand.

internal branding

The process of convincing all of an organization's employees and internal stakeholders to embrace the brand insight and adopt the identity and processes that will create the brand experience.

line extension

See brand extension

logo

A symbolic graphical representation consisting of a stylized word, pictogram, or both, that stands for the whole brand identity and distinguishes the brand from its competition and from generic products. When animated, it is sometimes referred to as an avatar. When legally protected, the name and logo together are called a trademark. In the automobile industry, the quaint term marque also persists.

Nation branding

The process of developing a coherent and consistent brand identity for an entire country, usually led by a government agency of that country, such as its tourism board. This is useful not only in attracting investment and tourism (*see* destination branding), but also in adding value to the country's exports. For example, French wines sell better than, say, Hungarian wines largely due to their superior branding.

marque

See logo

permission marketing

A theory in which customers willingly accede to certain marketing communications, for example, by signing up to receive e-mails, thereby making the marketer's message far more compelling.

positioning

The process of strategically maneuvering a brand into a certain position in the customer's mind, particularly in relation to other brands in the same or similar categories. A brand can also be positioned as the first in a new category. The most effective positioning implicitly repositions competing brands into a disadvantage.

slogan

See claim

storytelling

Creating a myth or background story to support a brand. This can be a simple reference to an archetype or commonly recognized cultural code; it does not have to involve a complete narrative.

strapline

See claim

tagline

See claim

touchpoint

See brand experience

trade dress

The sum of the elements of a package or label design which can be considered part of the intellectual property of a brand identity, and legally protected along with the name and logo.

trademark

See logo

tribal brand

See cult brand

Bibliography

Books

There are a lot of books about branding. Some deal with the subject directly, others in the context of advertising, graphic design, PR, marketing, or another subject.

The following list—which just scratches the surface—offers a starting point for readers seeking perspectives on the issues and current thinking in the practice of branding. Most of these authors have decades of experience, and much valuable wisdom to impart. Where relevant, I have cited some of the works below in the course of this book.

David Aaker. *Brand Portfolio Strategy.* **Free Press, 2004**
The latest of several influential books from one of the leading authorities on branding, this book lays out the science of bringing order to any brand menagerie.

Allen P. Adamson. *Brand Simple.* **Palgrave Macmillan, 2006**
The managing director of Landor explains how brands succeed by integrating strategy, identity, and internal branding to motivate employees and ambassadors.

Tom Asacker. *A Clear Eye for Branding.* **Paramount Market Publishing, 2005**
One of the first to point out that branding is a two-way street: a company must listen to how customers define its brand and constantly work to keep them satisfied, if it wants the brand to thrive.

Douglas Atkin. *The Culting of Brands. Portfolio, 2004*
Draws a parallel between brand affiliation and cult affiliation. The comparison allows for some interesting insights into how enormously popular brands like Apple, Nike, and Harley-Davidson gain and keep the unswerving loyalty of their die-hard devotees.

Scott Bedbury. *A New Brand World.* **Viking, 2001**
Priceless wisdom from the man who led not one great company but two—Nike and Starbucks—to the pinnacle of brand marketing. Bedbury's lesson is that these two brands are not exceptional; they're regular, solid brands built through years of hard work.

Phil Dusenberry. *Then We Set His Hair on Fire. Portfolio, 2005*
Drawing on his years as a senior advertising executive, the tales of this former BBDO chairman contain many wise lessons about brand insight and ideas.

The Economist. *Brands and Branding.* **Bloomberg Press, 2004**
A compendium of essays and white papers on the science, if not the art, of branding. Seventeen leading brains share know-how on the methods and business rationales for building effective brands. Required reading for MBAs.

Seth Godin. *All Marketers Are Liars.* **Portfolio, 2005**
"Marketers aren't liars. They are just storytellers. It's the consumers who lie to themselves every day. Successful marketers are just the providers of stories that consumers choose to believe." In his casual, humorous style, Godin, a popular American marketing guru, shares his pithy thoughts about consumer behavior and how brands cater to it through storytelling. Also try *Purple Cow* and *Small is the New Big.*

Philip Kotler and Waldemar Pfoertsch. *B2B Brand Management.* **Springer, 2006**
Even in business-to-business marketing, the brand is vital. Differentiation, positioning,and customer responsiveness are as critical in B2B as they are in any other area.

Martin Lindstrom. *Brand Sense.* **Free Press, 2005**
The Danish brand guru espouses his ideas on addressing all the senses, not just vision and hearing, in building a satisfying brand experience.

Margaret Mark and Carol Pearson. *The Hero and the Outlaw: Building Brands Through the Power of Archetypes.* **McGraw-Hill, 2001**
Explores the idea that brands, and customers' responses to brands, conform to Jungian archetypes residing in the unconscious, and how to use those archetypes to build compelling brands.

William J. McEwen. *Married to the Brand.* **Gallup Press, 2005**
Drawing on decades of research, the author argues that a relationship with a brand is just like a relationship with a spouse—long-term, emotional, financial, and hard to get out of without a real sense of loss.

Marcello Minale. *How to Keep Running a Successful Design Company.* **Booth-Clibborn Editions, 1999**
One of Minale's last books, this is filled with his advice on life, business, and his irrepressible philosophy of design. Sadly out of print and hard to find. Look for other books by Minale Tattersfield: *Leader of the Pack, All Together Now, How to Design a Successful Petrol Station.*

Marty Neumeier. *The Brand Gap.* **New Riders Press, 2003**
A fine exploration of the problems many old brands have in keeping up with customers' changing tastes and shifting allegiances. A brand must wrap up the emotional and rational, strategy and execution, in order to gain customers' loyalty.

Wally Olins. *On Brand.* **Thames & Hudson, 2004**
A charming and witty introduction to branding and how it works, by the eminence grise of brand identity. A must.

Robert L. Peters. *Worldwide Identity: Inspired Design from 40 Countries.* Rockport, 2005
An exhaustive look at the state of brand identity around the globe, and a great jumping-off point for anyone looking to expand their horizons in global branding.

Clotaire Rapaille. *The Culture Code.* Broadway, 2006
Love him or hate him, Rapaille's ideas have been enormously influential in America's corporate world. Though he is often accused of oversimplifying cultural nuances and complexities, his conclusion that consumer behavior is driven by base, "reptilian" urges has a lot of empirical support.

Al Ries and Laura Ries. *The Fall of Advertising and the Rise of PR.* HarperCollins, 2002
The Rieses make the argument that public relations, because its methods are not as obvious to the public, can be more effective than advertising at planting brand insights in people's heads. Also look for *22 Immutable Laws of Branding,* in which the father–daughter duo continue their "Immutable Laws" series.

Al Ries and Jack Trout. *Positioning.* McGraw-Hill, 2001
A seminal book in marketing thought whose title became a part of the branding lexicon (parts of this book were originally published in the early 1970s). Explains how a brand can occupy the most desirable position in everyone's minds vis-à-vis the competition.

Kevin Roberts. *Lovemarks.* powerHouse Books, 2004
A convincing call to rethink brands as objects of love and devotion. Though he's a tireless self-promoter, Roberts' insights are groundbreaking.

Randall Rothenberg. *Pentagram v. Monacelli,* 1999
A retrospective of work by the partners of the legendary design collective. Provocative and inspiring, as expected.

Bill Schley and Carl Nichols, Jr. *Why Johnny Can't Brand.* Portfolio, 2005
Includes some hilarious examples of dot-com companies that mistook a crazy ad campaign for a brand, and some sobering caveats about what it takes to build a real brand, as opposed to merely a funny ad.

Jack Trout. *Big Brands, Big Trouble.* Wiley, 2001
The bigger you are, the harder you fall. Mega-brands can achieve mega-success; but juggernauts are hard to steer, and often go off track, victims of their own size.

James Twitchell. *Twenty Ads that Shook the World.* Crown, 2000; Three Rivers Press, 2001
Professor Twitchell, one of the foremost scholars of advertising, reaches back to the early twentieth century to bring useful historical perspective to a field whose long-term memory often seems limited to five minutes. A parade of classics.

James Twitchell. *Branded Nation.* Simon & Schuster, 2004
Many have observed that everything has a brand; Twitchell is able to explain, lucidly and at length, how noncommercial organizations such as churches, universities, nonprofits, and others build and exploit their brands through storytelling.

Web resources
There are several good websites on branding, some of which allow visitors to post questions about branding and get answers from real humans in a fairly short amount of time, free of charge. More recently, there has been a proliferation of blogs on branding, some of which are better, and last longer, than others.

Allaboutbranding.com A New Zealand-based site with many white papers and other resources.

Brandchannel.com Weekly articles, debates, and forums, managed by Interbrand, but with an independent spirit.

Brandscape.co.ke A strong African perspective from this site based in Kenya. Valuable insights for anyone managing a brand in an up-and-coming market.

Brandweek.com Companion to the magazine (sister publication of Adweek and PRweek), requires a paid subscription to use all the site's resources.

Designcouncil.org.uk An advisory and educational board, funded by the British government to promote design. Look for the case studies.

DMI.org The Design Management Institute, based in Boston, offers a rich variety of professional resources, such as case studies, to paid members. Casual visitors to the site will also find useful information, free.

Luxist.com All about luxury brands.

MarketingProfs.com This extensive forum on all manner of marketing topics can be an invaluable resource for anyone starting out in branding.

MediaBistro.com A website devoted to all things media-related, including branding. Free resources include job searching, discussion forums, and extensive archives.

WonderBranding Thoughts on defining brands for women, by women (michelemiller.blogs.com/marketing_to_women).

Index

Credits

New City College
Library and Learning Centre

302465

I'd like to thank the following people who, each in his or her own way, helped make this book a little better.

First and foremost, I'd like to thank Lindy Dunlop, my editor and mentor at RotoVision, and the rest of the team for their vision and faith. Without them, this project would never even have begun!

All those who took the time and effort to help me assemble the material for this book. You know who you are; your names and work appear throughout these pages. Your contributions have been the *sine qua non*.

Barth Healey and Jane Thomas for encouragement and assistance in countless ways. You don't know how much I appreciate your support.

My teachers for the inspiration and encouragement they gave me when I was young and stupid. To my professors in media studies at NYU– Deirdre Boyle, Chyng-Fen Sun, and Kathleen Hulley– for their guidance and mentoring now that I am grown-up and stupid.

The terrific people at *The New York Times*, including Tom Bodkin, Margaret O'Connor, and Alan Robertazzi, to name just three. And a special shout-out to Nancy Weinstock and Phyllis Collazo for their help in finding images to use.

All those I've had the privilege of working with and learning from over the years, for pushing me ahead, each in their own unique way: Bill Anderson, Julia Tennant, Peter Phillips, Earl Powell, Anne Bouchenoir, Jean Bouchenoir, Robert Fridrich, Pavlina Safratova, Jan Safrata, Zuzana Rakusanova, Pavel Rakusan, Michal Richtr, Gilles Bérouard, Marek Sebestak, Martha Jane Pinder, Revan Schendler, David Gross, Marie D'Ippolito, Michael Gerbino, Martin Nissim, Tony Angotti, and Tom Thomas, who gave me my first real job.

And my brother Adam, for bugging me about what I was going to do next…